FEAST OF FLAVOURS
from the Chinese Kitchen

FEAST OF **FLAVOURS**
from the
Chinese
Kitchen

A STEP-BY-STEP CULINARY ADVENTURE

mc **Marshall Cavendish**
Cuisine

The Publisher wishes to thank Robinson & Co., (Singapore) Pte Ltd for the loan of their crockery and utensils.

Project Editor: Jamilah Mohd Hassan
Editor: Yeo Puay Khoon/Illydea Seulasteri Ishak
Designer: Ang Lee Ming/Jailani Basari
Photographer: Sam Yeo
Production Co-ordinator: Nor Sidah Haron
Food Preparation: Sharon Soh

© 2005 Marshall Cavendish International (Asia) Private Limited

Published by Marshall Cavendish Cuisine
An imprint of Marshall Cavendish International (Asia) Private Limited
A member of the Times Publishing Limited
Times Centre, 1 New Industrial Road, Singapore 536196
Tel: (65) 6213 9288   Fax: (65) 6285 4871
E-mail: te@sg.marshallcavendish.com
Online Bookstore: www.marshallcavendish.com/genref

Malaysian Office:
Marshall Cavendish (Malaysia) Sdn Bhd (3024-D)
(General & Reference Publishing)
(Formerly known as Federal Publications Sdn Berhad)
Times Subang, Lot 46, Persiaran Teknologi Subang
Subang Hi-Tech Industrial Park
Batu Tiga, 40000 Shah Alam
Selangor Darul Ehsan, Malaysia
Tel: (603) 5635 2191, 65628 6888   Fax: (603) 5635 2706
E-mail: cchong@my.marshallcavendish.com

National Library Board Singapore Cataloguing in Publication Data

Nguyen Thanh Diep.
Feast of flavours from the Chinese kitchen : a step-by-step culinary adventure / Nguyen Thanh Diep.
– Singapore : Marshall Cavendish Cuisine,- c2005.
p. cm. – (Feast of flavours)
Includes index.
ISBN : 981-232-673-1

1. Cookery, Chinese. I. Title. II. Series: Feast of flavours

TX724.5.C5
641.5951 – dc21   SLS2005018831

Printed in Singapore by Times Graphics Pte Ltd

Contents

COOKING TECHNIQUES

Chinese cooking has developed numerous cooking methods to make the most out of the variety of foods and ingredients available in the vast country. Ingredients and methods vary from region to region and often, there will be regional differences in the preparation of the same dishes.

Basic techniques of Chinese cooking include precooking techniques such as parboiling and partial frying and cooking techniques such as frying, sautéing, braising, stewing, boiling, simmering, steaming, "flavour-potting" and smoking.

Precooking methods

Precooking meats gets rid of off-odours while precooking vegetables gets rid of astringency or bitterness and highlights their fresh colour. Usually, ingredients are either parboiled or partially fried first before they are combined with other ingredients.

Parboiling

There are four methods of parboiling, namely parboiling, slow-boiling, hot-plunging or blanching, and quick-boiling. Each method produces a different result.

Parboiling

Vegetables such as taro root, Chinese yams and fresh bamboo shoots have to be parboiled by cooking in boiling water to remove their astringent taste. Parboiling also makes peeling much easier.

Slow-boiling

Slow-boiling is used to prepare ingredients that have a longer cooking time than other ingredients in the same recipe, such as pork tripe. To slow-boil, simmer the ingredient in boiling water until tender then add to the rest of the ingredients.

Hot-plunging or blanching

Hot-plunging or blanching is used to retain the colour and texture of tender and fresh vegetables, such as celery, spinach and green beans. First plunge vegetables into a pot of boiling water and remove when the water starts to boil again. Drain and run under cold water immediately.

Quick-boiling

Quick-boiling can get rid of the blood odour and small bits of bone from the meat. To quick-boil meat, place the meat in cold water and bring to the boil. Remove and drain once the water starts to boil. To quick-boil pig kidney, fish and chicken, plunge into boiling water and remove once it is cooked.

Partial frying

There are two methods of partial frying in Chinese cooking.

Sliding through the oil

Sliding through the oil means placing an ingredient in warm oil at 70-100°C (160–210°F) for just long enough to seal in the juices.

Going through the oil

Going through the oil means deep-frying an ingredient, usually a meat, in hot oil at 110–170°C (230–340°F) until partially or thoroughly cooked, depending on what is desired.

Cooking temperatures

Temperature control is an essential technique in Chinese cooking because different temperatures and cooking times produce different results.

In Chinese recipes, there are three kinds of heat: high heat, used in stir-frying, quick-frying and deep-frying; medium heat, used in sautéing, slippery-frying and deep-frying coated food; and low heat, used in steaming, simmering, braising and stewing.

High heat is used for producing a fast boil, where the water or liquid is kept bubbling, for hot-plunging and quick-boiling. It is also used for reducing broths and stocks.

Medium heat is used for keeping liquids at a moderate boil in some types of braising.

Low heat is used for keeping liquids at a slow boil or at a simmer during stewing, simmering and "flavour-potting".

Cooking with oil

Oil is warm when no bubbles appear around a small piece of vegetable leaf or a slice of ginger that has been tossed into the oil.

Oil is moderately hot when small bubbles sizzle around a piece of ginger that has been tossed into the oil.

Oil is very hot when a 3-cm (1-in) cube of day-old bread turns brown in 1 minute when dropped into the oil.

Oil is boiling hot when a heavy haze appears and the oil bubbles vigorously.

Most recipes require either hot or very hot oil. Oil at lower temperatures are used for partial frying while extremely hot oil is used for crisping and browning coated foods that have already been fried at a lower temperature.

Coating

There are a few types of coating used in Chinese cooking. The most common one is made of two parts cornstarch and one part water. It is usually used in slippery-frying and deep-frying.

Other popular coatings include an egg and breadcrumb coating and a flour and egg yolk coating. These 2 coatings require two-step preparation. For the former, dip into beaten egg yolk then roll in breadcrumbs. For the latter, dip into flour then into beaten egg yolk.

COOKING TECHNIQUES

Stir-frying

Stir-frying is one of the most famous methods of Chinese cooking but it is also the most difficult because speed and control is critical in ensuring success.

In stir-frying, food is cooked quickly at high temperatures in order to preserve its natural colour and texture, especially vegetables. Stir-frying meat seals in the juices prior to further cooking. It is a healthy method of cooking since very little oil is used.

When stir-frying, make sure that you use a good source of heat that can be easily adjusted. The gas cooker is recommended for its ease of control and practicality. On the other hand, electric hot plates are unsuitable for stir-frying because of poor heat control.

Important notes to remember:

1. Prepare all ingredients before starting to stir-fry.
2. Cut ingredients into similar sized small cubes or slices so that they cook quickly and evenly.
3. Heat the wok before adding oil and make sure that the oil is really hot before you add the ingredients.
4. To flavour the oil, fry garlic and shallots until fragrant and light browned before adding the remaining ingredients.
5. Stir ingredients constantly to ensure even cooking.
6. Be careful not to overcook.
7. Use simple garnishes.

Boiling (Poh, Sap and Luk)

Boiling may seem to be the simplest cooking method but in Chinese cooking, there are as many as three different degrees of boiling, namely Poh, Sap and Luk. The most commonly used one is Poh, where a plentiful amount of stock or water is rapidly boiled for a brief period. The heat is then reduced to allow it to simmer for a couple of hours. A considerable amount of stock or water is left behind, unlike in braising and stewing. Poh is used for making porridge, rice and soups but when cooking rice, you have to cook until all the liquid is absorbed by the rice.

Sap is done by placing meat into rapidly boiling water briefly. Sometimes, the meat is allowed to cook further by leaving it in the hot water with the heat turned off. The cooked meat can be served marinated, covered with a sauce or with a dip. Getting the right timing is critical to the success of this method, and anybody who has tried preparing "Hainanese Chicken Rice" will definitely attest to that.

The third variation is Luk, which is mainly used for cooking green leafy vegetables and noodles by scalding quickly in boiling water or stock. All sorts of green leafy vegetables can be cooked this way then mixed with oil and sauces, preserving their natural crunchiness. Noodles can also be prepared with this method, then either mixed with sauce and served with meat on top or served in soup. Luk softens egg noodles and gets rid of excess starch prior to stir-frying.

Meat, cut into small pieces or shredded to ensure adequate scalding, can also be prepared in this way. When scalded properly, the flavour and marinade will be sealed inside. This method is useful for preparing meat for soups so that scum will not form.

Important notes to remember:

1. Use a wok or pot that can contain enough water to immerse the food. The water must be boiling before the food is added.
2. Watch the duration of cooking time and adjust heat accordingly to avoid overcooking.
3. When boiling for a long duration, make sure that there is adequate water or stock in the pot. Top up accordingly if needed.

4. To prevent vegetables or noodles from overcooking, use a wire mesh ladle to scoop them out of the pot quickly.
5. After vegetables and noodles are done, quickly plunge into cold water to stop cooking then drain well. This helps to retain the fresh green colour of the vegetables.
6. Garnish boiled dishes simply with some chopped spring onions, coriander leaves and chillies.

Shallow-frying

When shallow-frying, the food is cooked with a small amount of oil and the food is hardly moved around so as to produce a crispy outer layer while keeping the inside moist. The natural flavour is also retained. This method is used for cooking fish, eggs, dumplings, stuffed vegetables and any foods that cook easily. Food prepared this way is usually served with a variety of dips and garnished with colourful vegetables and fruits to make the plain fried dish more attractive.

Use a flat pan for shallow-frying so that the oil can be evenly spread out and heated up before adding the food. This prevents food from sticking. Control the temperature and watch the timing carefully to prevent overcooking. Start by cooking on high heat for a few seconds, then turn down to medium or low heat, depending on the thickness of the food.

Deep-frying

To deep-fry food, the food has to be immersed in very hot oil. This produces a very crispy outside, especially when cooking poultry and seafood. Deep-fried food can either be marinated or coated with a batter, then served with a dip or covered with a cooked sauce.

To prevent overcooking, carefully regulate the temperature and observe the timing of the cooking period. Use a wok for deep-frying so that the food can be totally immersed in oil or partly immersed with enough room for basting.

Steaming

To steam food, place the food above boiling water and let the heat from the steam cook the food. It is an easy, fast and clean method of cooking. Although the method is simple, the correct marinade has to be carefully chosen to produce the desired flavour and texture.

Steaming is good for meat, fish and prawn dishes. When done, add garnishing to bring out the flavour and make the dish more attractive. You can use garnishings such as red chilli flowers, spring onions soaked in cold water for curling effect or a bunch of coriander leaves to make the dish more colourful.

Important notes to remember:

1. Use a metal steamer with a tight-fitting lid. Make sure the steamer is big enough for the food. The amount of water required depends on the length of steaming period but as a general guide, fill the steamer up to the halfway mark of the bottom pan. Top up with boiling water accordingly when there is not enough water to finish the steaming.
2. Make sure that the water in the steamer is at a rapid boil before putting in the food.
3. Whenever the cover is opened, wipe the underside dry to prevent condensed water from dripping onto the food. Alternatively, a dry towel can be placed under the lid to prevent dripping.
4. All meat and seafood should be marinated before steaming, for at least 15 minutes. When using a thickening, always stir the food again just before steaming to prevent lumps from forming.
5. When steamed for the correct length of time, the resulting texture will be very smooth. Oversteamed egg dishes will produce watery, coarse and pockmarked texture.

There is another method of steaming called 'double steaming' or 'closed steaming'. The difference is that the steaming is done in a closed stoneware pot. Sometimes, the Chinese will scoop out the insides of whole coconuts, winter melons and pumpkins so that they can be used as pots to prepare herbal soups with added flavour. This method is mainly used for preparing herbal soups, usually with expensive herbs and ingredients.

Braising and Stewing

This is a long cooking process which takes up to several hours. Meat, seafood and vegetables are slowly simmered together with a variety of sauces and spices to create delicious Chinese dishes with rich sauces and wonderful aromas.

The success of braising and stewing depends on the combination of sauces, ingredients and spices used. Light and thick soy sauces are essential ingredients. Ginger, garlic and shallots give flavour while popular spices used include five-spice powder, cinnamon, clove, star anise and Szechuan and white peppercorns. It is a good idea to wrap all the spices in a muslin bag so that the spices can be easily removed as required and prevent the spices from clouding the sauce.

Before braising, make sure the meat has been marinated for some time so that it can absorb all the seasoning. You can also seal in flavour and juices of meat and vegetables by frying quickly in oil or by blanching in boiling water. Keep the garnishing very simple for braised dishes, some chopped spring onion or topping of coriander or parsley will suffice.

Usually, the earthen pot or clay pot is used because of they are better for slow cooking. The wok is also used, especially for whole fowls, fish and large cuts of meat. When braising, applying too much heat will ruin the dish. It is easier to use an electric crockpot for braising and stewing.

Roasting and Grilling

Traditionally, roasting in Chinese cooking is done either on an open or closed spit. Nowadays, the conventional oven is used. Chinese roasted pig, duck and goose with crispy skin and tasty meat are famous all over the world. For the best roasted meats, you have to use a closed, turning drum-shaped spit that is fired by charcoal. A variation is dry-roasting in a wok filled with coarse salt. This method is used to make "Salt Baked Chicken", a delicious chicken dish with a simple seasoning.

The Chinese are also famous for their grilled meats, especially grilled pork and grilled spareribs. For the best grilled meats, you have to grill on an open spit fired by charcoal. Alternatively, an electric grill or turbo broiler can be used.

Important notes to remember:

1. Choose the correct cut of meat.
2. Allow enough time for meat to marinate. When marinating large chunks of meat, prick with a fork so that the marinade can penetrate more effectively.
3. Always preheat the oven, grill or broiler before putting in the meat. The high heat will cook the outside of the meat very quickly and seal in the juices and flavour of the meat. Watch the timing carefully to prevent overcooking.
4. As the meat is cooking, brush with some melted fat to keep it moist. Put a pan below the meat to catch any drippings which can be used as a basting liquid or as a sauce.

Smoking

Smoking adds fragrance and flavour to the meat. The meat is often partially cooked first by steaming, then cured in smoke from burning camphor wood, tea leaves or peanut shells. Smoking is usually done in a pot or a wok. Poultry is usually deep-fried after smoking to obtain the crispy skin, so well-loved by the Chinese.

COOKING UTENSILS

Ladle or Spatula
The long ladle or spatula is best for cooking with the wok. When using an iron wok, you can use a metal spatula but a wooden spatula is needed when using a non-stick wok to prevent scratching.

Wok
The wok is usually made of black cast iron or steel so it absorbs varying degrees of heat very quickly. Some woks are coated with non-stick material (teflon) so they are easier to clean and reduce oil splatter from cooking. Flat bottomed woks are also available nowadays for cooking on electric plates. A wok cover can also be used to reduce cooking time and to prevent excessive reduction of liquid.

A wok should be seasoned properly before use. To season, wash the wok and dry it well then oil the surface by rubbing it with a little cooking oil. Heat up the wok then let it cool down. Repeat these steps for another 2-3 times, then wipe the wok with kitchen paper or cloth.

To clean the wok, place it under running water while it is still hot and brush off dirt. If using a non-stick wok, clean with a soft sponge instead. Avoid using harsh detergents to clean the wok. After cleaning, make sure that the wok is completely dry by wiping dry or heating up the wok.

Chopping block
The Chinese chopping block is usually round in shape, at least a few inches thick and quite heavy. Its heavy weight makes it ideal when chopping with a heavy cleaver, since the ingredients will not slip or move. After use, scrape the surface with the cleaver, brush with a wire mesh then wash and wipe dry. Never soak the chopping block in water. You should sun it occasionally to prevent an odour.

Claypot

Claypots are good for slow cooking methods such as braising and stewing because heat is absorbed and evenly distributed. There is also less evaporation as compared to other types of cooking pots and saucepans. As a result, meat, rice and porridge cooked in claypots taste more flavoursome.

After cooking, food can be served straight from the claypot. The food will be kept warm for a long time because the claypot can retain heat very well. Claypots are available in Chinese sundry shops and in a wide range of sizes.

Steamers

Metal steamers are made up of a bottom section for holding water, a top section for placing perforated trays and a cover on top. Steam passes through the holes to cook the food. These steamers are readily available at Chinese sundry shops. A wok can also be used for steaming, as long as you have a tall cover and a steamer stand to hold the food above the water. For steaming breads and dumplings, bamboo steamers are used to prevent water from collecting and dripping onto the food.

When steaming food, remember to bring the water to the boil before putting in the food.

Chinese cleaver

The Chinese cleaver is used for chopping, cutting, slicing, mincing and shredding. Its flat side can also be used for crushing garlic. Choose a good heavy cleaver made of carbon steel that will be suitable for most purposes.

Sharpen with a whetstone regularly.

Wire mesh ladle

The Chinese wire mesh ladle with a wooden handle is usually used for scalding noodles. It is also useful for scooping up food during deep-frying. They are available in a variety of sizes but a 15-cm (6-in) diameter one should be appropriate for the home kitchen.

WEIGHTS & MEASURES

Quantities for this book are given in Metric and American (spoon and cup) measures. Standard spoon and cup measurements used are: 1 teaspoon = 5 ml, 1 dessertspoon = 10 ml, 1 tablespoon = 15 ml, 1 cup = 250 ml. All measures are level unless otherwise stated.

DRY MEASURES

Metric	Imperial
30 grams	1 ounce
45 grams	$1^1/_2$ ounces
55 grams	2 ounces
70 grams	$2^1/_2$ ounces
85 grams	3 ounces
100 grams	$3^1/_2$ ounces
110 grams	4 ounces
125 grams	$4^1/_2$ ounces
140 grams	5 ounces
280 grams	10 ounces
450 grams	16 ounces (1 pound)
500 grams	1 pound, $1^1/_2$ ounces
700 grams	$1^1/_2$ pounds
800 grams	$1^3/_4$ pounds
1 kilogram	2 pounds, 3 ounces
1.5 kilograms	3 pounds, $4^1/_2$ ounces
2 kilograms	4 pounds, 6 ounces

LENGTH

Metric	Imperial
0.5 cm	$^1/_4$ inch
1 cm	$^1/_2$ inch
1.5 cm	$^3/_4$ inch
2.5 cm	1 inch

LIQUID AND VOLUME MEASURES

Metric	Imperial	American
5 ml	$^1/_6$ fl oz	1 teaspoon
10 ml	$^1/_3$ fl oz	1 dessertspoon
15 ml	$^1/_2$ fl oz	1 tablespoon
60 ml	2 fl oz	$^1/_4$ cup (4 tablespoons)
85 ml	21/2 fl oz	$^1/_3$ cup
90 ml	3 fl oz	$^3/_8$ cup (6 tablespoons)
125 ml	4 fl oz	$^1/_2$ cup
180 ml	6 fl oz	$^3/_4$ cup
250 ml	8 fl oz	1 cup
300 ml	10 fl oz (1/2 pint)	$1^1/_4$ cups
375 ml	12 fl oz	$1^1/_2$ cups
435 ml	14 fl oz	$1^3/_4$ cups
500 ml	16 fl oz	2 cups
625 ml	20 fl oz (1 pint)	$2^1/_2$ cups
750 ml	24 fl oz ($1^1/_5$ pints)	3 cups
1 litre	32 fl oz ($1^3/_5$ pints)	4 cups
1.25 litres	40 fl oz (2 pints)	5 cups
1.5 litres	48 fl oz ($2^2/_5$ pints)	6 cups
2.5 litres	80 fl oz (4 pints)	10 cups

OVEN TEMPERATURE

Regulo	°C	°F	Gas
Very slow	120	250	1
Slow	150	300	2
Moderately slow	160	325	3
Moderate	180	350	4
Moderately hot	190/200	370/400	5/6
Hot	210/220	410/440	6/7
Very hot	230	450	8
Super hot	250/290	475/550	9/10

ABBREVIATION

Tbsp	tablespoon
dsp	dessertspoon
tsp	teaspoon
kg	kilogram
g	gram
l	litres
ml	mililitres

STARTERS

Beat mixture against a bowl continuously for 1 minute to tenderise meat.

After shaping into a long roll, use a pastry cutter to divide dough into 18 equal pieces.

Pinch along the seam to seal dumpling into

FRIED MEAT AND VEGETABLE DUMPLINGS

Meat and vegetable pastry served with vinegar and ginger dip.

Ingredients

Minced pork with a little fat or chicken	180 g (6 oz)
White cabbage (pak choy)	2 leaves, about 120 g (4 oz), finely chopped
Chinese chives	30 g (1 oz), finely chopped
Spring onion (scallion)	1, finely chopped
Cooking oil	2 Tbsp
Fresh chicken stock	185 ml (¾ cup)

Seasoning Ingredients

Sugar	1 tsp
Salt	¾ tsp
Pepper	¼ tsp
Light soy sauce	1 tsp
Chinese rice wine	1 tsp
Sesame oil	1 tsp
Cooked or shallot oil	1 Tbsp

Pastry

Plain (all-purpose) flour	120 g (4 oz)
Salt	¼ tsp
Boiling water	165 ml (⅔ cup)

Vinegar and Ginger Dip

Vinegar	2 Tbsp
Sugar	1 tsp
Ginger	30 g (1 oz), shredded

Method

- Season minced meat with seasoning ingredients and set aside.
- Place finely chopped cabbage in a muslin cloth and squeeze to remove excess vegetable liquid. Add to minced pork, together with chives and spring onion. Mix to a smooth paste.
- Lift mixture with the hand and slap it against a bowl or chopping board continuously for 1 minute to improve the texture of the meat.
- Refrigerate meat mixture for 1 hour.
- To make pastry, sieve flour into a mixing bowl and add salt. Pour boiling water into flour and quickly mix into a stiff dough with a spoon.
- Form dough into a round ball and leave to rest, covered with a dry towel, for 30 minutes.
- Knead dough on a lightly floured board for 3–5 minutes until smooth. Shape into a long sausage roll and divide equally into 18 pieces.
- Make each piece into a round ball and roll out into a thin circle (about 7-cm (3-in) diameter).
- Put 1 tsp of meat mixture, slightly off centre into each circle. Pleat one half of the wrapper and press against the unpleated side to seal and form a half-moon shape dumpling.
- Heat a flat pan with 2 Tbsp oil until hot, reduce heat and place dumplings in a circle close together.
- Fry for 1 minute until bottom of the dumpling is golden brown. Do not disturb the dumpling while frying.
- Pour chicken stock into the pan, cover and simmer dumplings on low heat for 4–5 minutes until cooked through.
- Drain off remaining liquid and transfer dumplings onto a serving dish.
- Serve hot with vinegar and ginger dip or chilli sauce.
- To prepare the vinegar and ginger dip, heat combined vinegar and sugar. Stir until sugar dissolves and pour immediately over ginger.
- Leave, covered, for 1–2 hours before serving.

DEEP-FRIED PORK ROLLS

Young bamboo shoots and Chinese mushrooms rolled in deep-fried pork make a tasty appetiser.

Ingredients

Boneless pork loin (*yok ngan*)	250 g (9 oz), half frozen to facilitate slicing
Carrot	5-cm (2-in) piece, peeled and cut into strips
Canned bamboo shoots	5-cm (2-in)piece, cut into strips
Dried Chinese mushrooms	2 large pieces, soaked and shredded
Breadcrumbs	45 g (1½ oz)
Oil	for deep-frying
Pineapple or cucumber slices	for garnishing

Seasoning Ingredients

Salt	½ tsp
Sugar	½ tsp
Pepper	¼ tsp
Chinese rice wine	2 tsp
Egg	1, beaten
Corn flour (cornstarch)	1 Tbsp

STEP-BY-STEP

After first slicing without cutting through, cut the subsequent slice completely through.

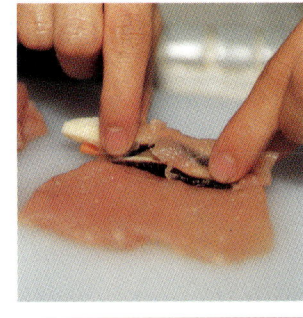

Spread each piece of meat out flat and place filling ingredients. Roll up meat to wrap filling ingredients.

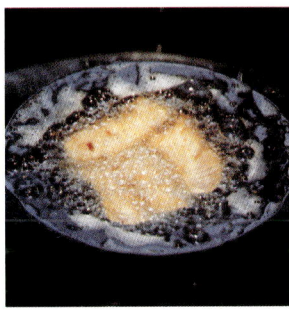

Heat up the wok and deep-fry pork rolls for about 5 minutes or until golden.

Method

- To double the size of the sliced meat so that it will be large enough to cover the vegetables, proceed in the following manner:
  Cut a 0.25-cm (¼ in) slice across the grain without cutting through. Cut the next slice completely through 0.25-cm (¼ in) from the first cut. Continue to cut in double slices on the whole piece of meat.

- Lightly bash each piece of meat with the blunt edge of a cleaver to tenderise. Marinate meat with seasoning ingredients for 30 minutes.
- Open and spread out each piece of meat on a flat surface and place 2 strips each of carrot, bamboo shoots and dried mushrooms.
- Roll up meat, enclosing vegetables. Coat well with breadcrumbs.

- Heat a wok with deep-frying oil. Deep-fry pork rolls for about 5 minutes or until golden. Drain from oil.
- Arrange on a serving dish and garnish with pineapple and cucumber slices.

STEAMED MUSHROOMS WITH PRAWN FILLING

Prawn-filled Chinese mushrooms served with a delicious chicken stock-based sauce.

Ingredients

Cooking oil	3 Tbsp
Dried Chinese mushrooms	12, soaked until soft and drained
Prawns (shrimps)	300 g (10 oz), shelled, deveined and minced
Water chestnuts	2, peeled and minced
Chinese sausage	1, sliced (optional)
Green peas	12
Egg white	1/2, beaten

Sauce Ingredients 'A' (combined)

Fresh chicken stock	250 ml (1 cup)
Salt	1/2 tsp
Pepper	1/2 tsp
Sugar	1/2 tsp
Sesame oil	1 tsp
Oyster sauce	1 tsp

Seasoning Ingredients

Salt	1/4 tsp
Pepper	1/4 tsp
Sugar	1/4 tsp
Corn flour (cornstarch)	1 tsp
Sesame oil	1/2 tsp
Egg white	1/2, lightly beaten, to be added last (reserve half portion for the sauce)

Sauce Ingredients 'B' (combined)

Reserved mushroom stock	185 ml (3/4 cup)
Chinese rice wine	1 tsp
Salt	1/4 tsp
Pepper	1/4 tsp
Sugar	1/4 tsp
Corn flour (cornstarch)	1 tsp

Using a pair of kitchen scissors, remove stems from Chinese mushrooms.

Fill mushrooms with prawn mixture then top with a green pea and sliced sausage.

Pour leftover liquid from steaming into combined sauce ingredients 'B'.

Method

- Heat wok with oil until hot and stir-fry mushrooms for 1–2 minutes. Add combined sauce ingredients 'A' and simmer for 5 minutes over low heat.
- Drain mushrooms from stock and allow to cool. Reserve stock for making sauce 'B'.
- Combine minced prawns with water chestnuts and stir in seasoning ingredients. Add beaten egg white and beat with a spoon until mixture is sticky.
- Stuff mushrooms with prawn mixture and press a green pea and 1 or 2 slices of sausage on each of the stuffed mushrooms. Steam over rapidly boiling water for 10 minutes.
- Remove from steamer and carefully pour liquid into combined sauce ingredients 'B'. Bring gravy to the boil. Reduce heat and simmer for 2–3 minutes. Add the reserved beaten egg white and pour over the mushrooms.

Cut a hole at the top of capsicum and remove all the seeds and pith. Take care to keep capsicum whole.

Fill up each capsicum completely with the mixture.

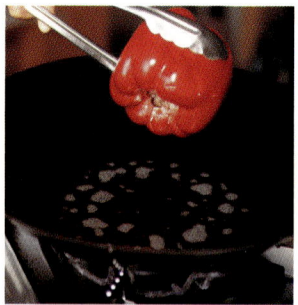

Using a pair of tongs, carefully lower stuffed capsicum into hot oil to fry, until slightly blistered.

S
T
E
P
-
B
Y
-
S
T
E
P

STUFFED CAPSICUMS

This colourful and tasty dish of red capsicums is garnished simply with coriander leaves.

Ingredients

Dried prawns (shrimps)	1$\frac{1}{2}$ Tbsp
Dried Chinese black mushrooms	8, medium
Red capsicums (bell peppers)	4, large
Lean pork	175–200 g (6$\frac{1}{2}$–7 oz)
Salt	1$\frac{1}{2}$ tsp
Soy sauce	2 Tbsp
Corn flour (cornstarch)	2 Tbsp
Vegetable oil	for deep-frying

Sauce Ingredients

Lard	15 g
Good stock	125 ml ($\frac{1}{2}$ cup)
Soy sauce	2 Tbsp
Oyster sauce	4 Tbsp
Corn flour (cornstarch)	2 Tbsp, mixed with 3 Tbsp water

Method

- Soak dried prawns and mushrooms for 20 minutes in a bowl of warm water.
- Meanwhile, remove the stems, all the seeds and any pith carefully from the capsicums through the hole at the top, making sure you keep them whole.
- Finely chop the pork. Drain and chop prawns and mushrooms (discarding hard stem tips) and add to pork. Stir in salt and soy sauce. Stuff mixture in each capsicum through the stem-hole, filling each one completely. Make a paste from corn flour mixed with 2 Tbsp water. Seal stuffing at the top of capsicums by spreading paste over the hole.

- Heat oil in a wok or deep-fat frier to 180°C (350°F); at this temperature a cube of stale bread will brown in 60 seconds. Lower capsicums, pasted-side down, into the oil one by one. Turn the heat to low and fry capsicums for 3–4$\frac{1}{2}$ minutes or until skins are softened and are slightly blistered.
- Remove capsicums from the oil and drain them. Cut each capsicum into 4 pieces and arrange them in a heatproof dish. Stand the dish on a trivet in a steamer and bring the water beneath to the boil. Cover and steam steadily for 15 minutes.

- Meanwhile heat lard in a wok or frying-pan over medium-low heat and add the rest of the sauce ingredients. Stir over high heat, for 1$\frac{1}{2}$–2 minutes until sauce thickens. Pour sauce over stuffed capsicums and serve immediately, from the heatproof dish.

Be careful when lifting bean curd sheets out after they have softened. Make sure you use both hands to spread them out and drain off water.

Shape filling into a sausage and place on bean curd sheet. Lift the edge of bean curd sheet to wrap over filling.

Roll up as tightly as possible. Use a pastry brush to apply some egg

DEEP-FRIED FIVE-SPICE ROLLS

This all-time favourite is usually served with ketchup, chilli sauce and soy-mustard dips.

Ingredients

Dried bean curd sheets	1 packet (225 g / 8 oz), 33 x 15-cm (13 x 6 in)
Pork with some fat in it	600 g (1 lb 5 oz), chopped into rice-sized bits
Spring onions (scallions)	12, the white part, cut into small rounds
Canned or fresh water chestnuts	175 g (6¹/₂ oz), peeled, chopped into rice-sized bits
Tapioca flour or potato flour	3 Tbsp
Egg yolks	2, medium-sized
Vegetable oil	for deep-frying
Tomato ketchup	to serve
Chilli sauce	to serve
Thick soy sauce	1 Tbsp, mixed with 1 tsp prepared hot mustard to serve

Marinade

Salt	1 tsp
Thin soy sauce	2 tsp
Sugar	2¹/₂ tsp
Shao Hsing wine or medium-dry sherry	5 tsp
Sesame oil	2 tsp
Five-spice powder	1 tsp
Egg whites	1¹/₂, medium-sized

Method

- Soak bean curd sheets in cold water for about 4 minutes or until sheets are soft and pliable. Lift each sheet carefully with both hands to drain, blot them with absorbent paper and place them flat on a large tea towel, one on top of another. Cover them with another tea towel to keep them just moist.
- Put finely chopped pork into a big bowl. Add the ingredients for the marinade, stir and leave for 5 minutes.
- Add spring onions and water chestnuts to the mixture. Stir in tapioca flour or potato flour, 1 Tbsp at a time, to ensure smooth mixing. Divide mixture into 16 portions.
- Take 1 bean curd sheet from the covered pile and put it on a flat surface with the long side next to you. Cut the sheet in half crossways.
- Scoop up a portion of the filling and roll it between your palms into the shape of a sausage. Place filling near the edge of the bean curd sheet and roll it away from you as tightly as possible.
- Using either your fingers or a pastry brush, smear some egg yolk on the opposite edge and seal roll. Leave the two ends open like a cigarette and place roll on a tray, sealed side down. Cover tray with a damp cloth. Repeat until all the sheets are filled.
- If you are using a wok for deep-frying, half-fill it with vegetable oil. If you are using a deep-fat frier, the oil should be 6- cm (1¹/₂-in) deep. Heat the oil to 190°C (375°F), at which temperature a cube of stale bread will brown in 50 seconds.
- Put in 8 rolls or however many will float freely in the oil. Deep-fry for 8 minutes or until milk chocolate-brown in colour. Remove them with a perforated ladle and drain on absorbent paper. Keep them warm. Repeat until all the rolls are done.
- Cut each roll into 5 pieces and put them on a large platter. Serve with the ketchup, chilli sauce and soy-mustard dips arranged on the table or in the middle of the platter.

Cut duck into 4 pieces for easy handling and cooking.

Squeeze out water from salted stems after soaking.

Add in tomatoes together with pepper and allow to simmer for another 10 minutes.

DUCK AND SALTED VEGETABLE SOUP

A simple savoury soup with duck and pickled plums.

Ingredients

Duck	$1/2$
Salted green stems (*harm choy*)	250 g (9 oz), cut into 5-cm (2-in) squares
Cooking oil	1 Tbsp
Ginger	5-cm (2-in) knob, crushed
Water	2.5 litres (10 cups)
Pickled sour plums (*sheen mui*)	2
Tomatoes	2, quartered
Pepper	$1/4$ tsp

Method

- Cut duck into 4 pieces and set aside.
- Soak salted stems in water for 1 hour. Drain and lightly squeeze out excess water.
- Heat oil in a pot and sauté ginger for 1–2 minutes until aromatic. Add duck and stir-fry for 5 minutes until the duck changes colour.
- Pour water into the pot and add salted stems and sour plums. Bring to the boil, reduce heat to low, cover and simmer for $2^1/_2$ hours or until duck is tender.
- Add tomatoes and pepper and simmer for a further 10 minutes.

OLD CUCUMBER AND PORK SOUP

A refreshing clear soup with a definite crunch to it.

Ingredients

Old cucumber with skin	1 large
Lean pork with fat	360 g (12 oz), whole piece, uncut and rinsed
Dried Chinese red dates	6, seeded and rinsed
Water	1.25 litres (5 cups)
Salt	1½ tsp
Light soy sauce	2 Tbsp

S
T
E
P
-
B
Y
-
S
T
E
P

Use a spoon to scoop out all the seeds from old cucumber.

Add dates to the soup pot then cover and boil all the ingredients together.

While soup is simmering, make sure to remove surface scum when it has accumulated.

Method

- Cut old cucumber in half lengthways. Scoop out seeds with a spoon and cut each half into 5-cm (2-in) pieces.
- Place cucumber, whole pork and water in a large pot. Add dates to the pot. Cover and bring to the boil.
- Add salt, reduce heat and simmer for 45–60 minutes. Skim off the surface scum from time to time.
- When pork is tender, remove and cut into 2-cm (1-in) thick slices. Return pork to soup.
- Serve with a small dish of light soy sauce as a dip for the pork.

BEAN CURD HOT POT

This popular Chinese soup is made with minced chicken, bean curd and bamboo shoots.

Ingredients

Soft bean curd	6 pieces or 6 packets silken soft bean curd
Chicken	60 g (2 oz), minced
Egg yolks	3
Salt	to taste
Pepper	to taste
Lard	2 tsp
Tender tips of winter bamboo shoot	30 g (1 oz)
Chicken stock	1.5 litres (6 cups)
Salt	to taste
Lettuce leaves	a few, torn into large pieces

S T E P - B Y - S T E P

Use a spoon to press bean curd through a sieve to make into a paste.

Pour egg yolk mixture into bean curd and chicken mixture. Mix until well combined.

Cover then steam mixture at high heat for 7 minutes.

Method

- Pass bean curd through a sieve. Mix with minced chicken.
- Beat egg yolks with salt and pepper. Add to bean curd and chicken mixture and blend well.
- Pour mixture into a mould lightly greased with lard. Steam over high heat for 7 minutes before serving.
- Meanwhile, add bamboo shoot tips to chicken stock and boil for 10 minutes. Season to taste.
- Put steamed mixture into a big soup bowl and pour boiling hot stock over. Add lettuce leaves.

Cut bean curd into small cubes.

After adding in green peas, allow to simmer for another 5 minutes.

Add in lightly beaten eggs as a final step.

HOT SOUR SOUP

Chicken and prawns are added to this peppery chicken stock-based vegetable soup

Ingredients

Chicken drumstick	1, boned and cut into small cubes
Shelled small prawns (shrimps)	300 g (10 oz), diced (optional)
Fresh chicken stock	2.25 litres (9 cups)
Szechuan vegetable (char choy)	1 large piece, unwashed and diced
Carrot	1, peeled and diced
Dried Chinese mushrooms	4, soaked and diced
Button mushrooms	1/2 can, quartered
Straw mushrooms	1/2 can, quartered
Fresh baby corn	10 cobs, diced
Red chillies	3, split to remove seeds
Chinese black vinegar	165 ml (2/3 cup)
Soft bean curd	1 square piece, diced
Frozen green peas	100 g (31/2 oz), rinsed
Sweet potato flour	4 Tbsp, mixed with 125 ml (1/2 cup) chicken stock, strained
Eggs	2, lightly beaten

Seasoning Ingredients

Pepper	1 tsp
Salt	1 tsp
Corn flour (cornstarch)	1 tsp

Method

- Marinate chicken and prawns with seasoning ingredients for 15 minutes.
- Pour strained stock into a deep cooking pot and bring to the boil. Add Szechuan vegetable, carrot, all the mushrooms, corn, chillies and black vinegar. Allow to simmer for 10 minutes.
- Put in chicken and prawns and when mixture begins to boil, add bean curd and green peas. Simmer for another 5 minutes, then stir in strained sweet potato flour mixture and finally the beaten eggs.

Scoop 1 tsp of filling and place in the centre of wantan wrapper.

Wrap around filling and gather edges together. Press firmly to seal.

Pour stock over wantans and vegetables then serve with chopped spring onions as garnish.

PRAWN WANTAN SOUP

Prawn dumplings add a wonderful flavour to this clear soup.

Ingredients

Small shelled prawns (shrimps)	150 g (5 oz), minced
Pork	120 g (4 oz), minced
Fresh water chestnuts	3, finely minced
Dried Chinese mushrooms	2, soaked and finely minced
Egg white	1/2, beaten
Wantan wrappers	120 g (4 oz)
Cooking oil	1 Tbsp
Flowering cabbage (*choy sum*)	2 stalks, cut into 3 sections
Spring onions (scallions)	2, chopped

Seasoning Ingredients

Light soy sauce	1 tsp
Salt	1/2 tsp
Sugar	1/2 tsp
Pepper	1/4 tsp
Corn flour (cornstarch)	1 tsp

Stock Ingredients

Fresh anchovy, chicken or pork bone stock	1.5 litres (6 cups)
Salt	1 1/2 tsp
Sesame oil	1 tsp
Pepper	1/2 tsp

Method

- Mix prawns, pork, water chestnuts and mushrooms with egg white and seasoning ingredients and leave for 30 minutes.
- Put 1 tsp of mixture in the centre of each *wantan* wrapper. Wrap around filling and fold edges to seal.
- Boil a saucepan of water and add 1 Tbsp of oil. Drop *wantans* in boiling water and cook for 1 minute. Remove with a perforated ladle and place in a deep soup bowl. Scald mustard green in the same boiling water for 1 minute. Drain and arrange around the sides of the bowl.
- Bring stock ingredients to the boil. Pour over *wantans* and vegetables. Serve garnished with chopped spring onion.

Stir-fried Szechuan Style Squid

Chilli Oyster Crabs

Sea Bass with Spicy Black Vinegar Sauce

Butter Prawns with Toasted Coconut

Crab Omelette

Fried Oyster Fritters

Braised Fish with Black Bean Sauce

Claypot Fish Head

SEAFOOD

Carefully score the inside of squid body, taking care not to cut through completely.

Stir-fry garlic and hot bean paste in a wok until fragrant. Then add in celery and stir-fry.

To mix sauce with squid and chillies evenly, stir and turn to coat.

STIR-FRIED SZECHUAN STYLE SQUID

Large fresh squid stir-fried with hot bean paste, celery and chilli.

Ingredients

Fresh large squid	600 g (1 lb 4 oz), cleaned, score the inner body and cut into thick slices, about 2 x 5-cm (1 x 2 in)
Salt	$^1/_2$ tsp
Pepper	$^1/_2$ tsp
Cooking oil	3 Tbsp, preferably lard
Garlic	3 cloves, minced
Hot bean paste	1 Tbsp
Tender young celery	1 stalk, sliced
Red chillies	2, sliced

Sauce Ingredients (combined)

Fresh chicken stock or water	375 ml (1$^1/_2$ cup)
Light soy sauce	1 Tbsp
Chinese wine	1 Tbsp
Sesame oil	1 tsp
Sugar	1 tsp
Pepper	$^1/_4$ tsp
Salt	$^1/_4$ tsp
Corn flour (cornstarch)	2 tsp

Method

- Season squid with salt and pepper for 15 minutes. Blanch seasoned squid in boiling salted water for 30–60 seconds. Drain well.
- Heat wok with oil until hot and stir-fry garlic and hot bean paste until fragrant. Add celery and stir-fry for 1$^1/_2$ minutes.
- Stir in sauce ingredients and bring to the boil. When sauce thickens, add squid and chillies, and very briefly toss the mixture.
- Transfer to serving dish and serve hot.

CHILLI OYSTER CRABS

Delicious chilli crabs given a twist with oyster sauce and Chinese wine.

Ingredients

Crabs	3 kg (6 lb 9 oz)
Cooking oil	250 ml
Ginger	60 g, peeled and cut into strips
Garlic	7 cloves, peeled and sliced
Shallots	7, peeled and sliced
Red chillies	10, seeded, machine blended with 125 ml ($\frac{1}{2}$ cup) water
Eggs	5, beaten lightly
Spring onions (scallions)	6, cut into 5-cm (2-in) lengths
Coriander (cilantro) leaves	2 sprigs, cut into 5-cm (2-in) lengths

Sauce Ingredients

Chinese rice wine	3 Tbsp
Chilli sauce	3 Tbsp
Oyster sauce	4 Tbsp
Sugar	4 dsp
Sesame oil	1 tsp
Pepper	$\frac{1}{4}$ tsp

STEP-BY-STEP

When cleaning crabs, remove pincers and crack shell open with a nutcracker.

Add crabs to wok and stir with chillies, ginger, garlic and shallots.

When crabs turn to bright red in colour, add in lightly beaten eggs.

Method

- Clean crabs, remove and crack pincers with a crab cracker. Trim legs and cut into 4 pieces.
- Heat oil in a large wok and stir-fry ginger, garlic and shallots until fragrant. Put in chillies and fry for 2 minutes.
- Add crabs and stir briskly. Cover wok for approximately 4–5 minutes. Uncover and stir briskly once again, then add sauce ingredients. When crabs are bright red and nearly cooked, pour in beaten eggs. Add spring onions, stirring to mix with sauce.
- Dish out, garnish with coriander leaves and serve hot with rice or toasted bread.

SEA BASS WITH SPICY BLACK VINEGAR SAUCE

Fried sea bass served with black vinegar sauce and a dash of chilli.

Ingredients

Sea bass or any freshwater fish	500–600 g (1 lb 1$\frac{1}{2}$ oz–1 lb 5 oz)
Salt	1 tsp
Pepper	$\frac{1}{2}$ tsp
Corn flour (cornstarch)	for coating fish
Cooking oil	3 Tbsp for deep-frying
Cooking oil	2 Tbsp
Garlic	2 large cloves, peeled and thinly sliced
Fresh ginger root	2.5-cm (1-in) knob, peeled and thinly sliced
Red chilli	1
Spring onions (scallions)	2
Corn flour (cornstarch)	2 tsp, mixed with 2 Tbsp chicken stock or water

Sauce Ingredients (combined)

Chicken stock	165 ml ($\frac{2}{3}$ cup)
Light soy sauce	$\frac{3}{4}$ Tbsp
Thick soy sauce	$\frac{1}{4}$ tsp
Sugar	60 g
Black vinegar	2 Tbsp
Salt	a pinch

S T E P - B Y - S T E P

Cut a criss-cross pattern on fish to help it cook later.

Fry fish then turn and fry on the other side, until batter is golden brown.

Pour thickened sauce over fish just before serving.

Method

- Use a sharp knife and deeply score both sides of the fish, starting 4 cm (1$\frac{1}{2}$ cm) from the gill opening. Lightly cut a criss-cross pattern on the tail end.
- Marinate fish with salt and pepper and set aside for 15 minutes. Coat fish with corn flour, making sure to coat the slits.

- Heat 3 Tbsp of oil in a non-stick frying pan and fry fish on both sides, covered, until batter is crisp and golden brown (about 10 minutes). Place fish on serving dish.
- Reheat pan with 2 Tbsp cooking oil. Add garlic and ginger and stir-fry for

20 seconds until fragrant. Stir in chilli and sauce ingredients and bring to a rapid boil.
- Add spring onions. Thicken with corn flour mixture and pour sauce over fish.

Use a pair of kitchen scissors to snip off the feelers of large prawns.

Pour omelette ingredients into a frying pan to make a thin omelette.

Add toasted coconut, sugar, salt and bird's eye chillies to heated butter.

BUTTER PRAWNS WITH TOASTED COCONUT

Buttered shrimps tossed with toasted coconut is an unmistakably luscious dish.

Ingredients

Large prawns (shrimps)	500 g (1 lb 1¹/₂ oz), feelers trimmed
Salt	1 tsp
Pepper	¹/₂ tsp
Oil	for deep-frying
Butter	90 g (3 oz)
Pan-toasted grated coconut	60 g (2 oz), blended in electric blender
Sugar	2 tsp
Bird's eye chillies	10, finely sliced
Chopped spring onion (scallion) and coriander (cilantro) leaves	
Small lime	1, juice extracted

Omelette

Eggs	2, beaten
Light soy sauce	1 tsp
Salt	¹/₄ tsp
Pepper	¹/₂ tsp

Method

- Season prawns with ¹/₂ tsp salt and pepper for 30 minutes.
- Make a thin omelette with omelette ingredients and when it has cooled, chop finely. Set aside.
- Heat oil for deep-frying and fry seasoned prawns until just cooked. Drain from oil.
- Heat butter over low heat and put in toasted coconut, sugar, ¹/₂ tsp salt and bird's eye chillies. Toss well until fragrant and add finely chopped omelette, spring onion, coriander leaves and lime juice.

Bring oil to the boil then fry rice vermicelli for 2 seconds, until crisp. Drain with a perforated ladle.

Fry crabmeat mixture for 10 seconds then drain with a perforated ladle.

Add in rice wine after frying mixture briskly.

S
T
E
P
-
B
Y
-
S
T
E
P

CRAB OMELETTE

An exotic and tasty omelette is delightful when served on a bed of deep-fried vermicelli.

Ingredients

Crabmeat	350 g (12 oz)
Rice vermicelli	120 g (4 oz)
Oil	800 ml (3$\frac{1}{4}$ cups)
Egg whites	6
Winter bamboo shoots	360 g (12 oz), shredded
Corn flour (cornstarch)	1$\frac{1}{2}$ Tbsp
Chicken stock	50 ml ($\frac{1}{4}$ cup)
Sesame oil	$\frac{1}{4}$ tsp
Salt	$\frac{1}{2}$ tsp
Rice wine	1 tsp

Method

- Fry rice vermicelli in boiling oil for 2 seconds. Drain. Vermicelli should be white and crisp. (Do not wash vermicelli, use it straight from the packet for a crisp result.) Keep oil.
- Beat egg whites until stiff and mix it in a big bowl with crabmeat, bamboo shoots, half the corn flour, chicken stock, sesame oil and salt.
- Reheat oil until it boils. Fry mixture for 10 seconds. Drain. Put dry mixture back into the pan and fry briskly. Add rice wine.
- Mix remaining corn flour with 2 Tbsp water. Add to crabmeat to thicken it.
- Line a plate with crisp rice vermicelli and pour crab mixture on top just before serving.

FRIED OYSTER FRITTERS

A delightful dish of deep-fried oysters served with tomato sauce.

Ingredients

Oysters	450 g (1 lb), shelled
Self-raising flour	50 g (1¼ oz)
Plain (all-purpose) flour	110 g (4 oz)
Eggs	3, beaten lightly
Water	4 Tbsp
Pepper	a pinch
Salt	a pinch
Oil	2 Tbsp
Parsley	8 sprigs, broken into small sections
Tomato sauce	for serving

Scoop out 1 Tbsp of mixture with an oyster.

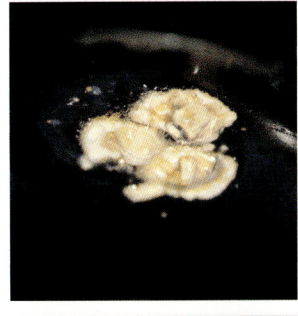

Drop the spoonful of mixture into a wok of hot oil and fry until it turns golden brown.

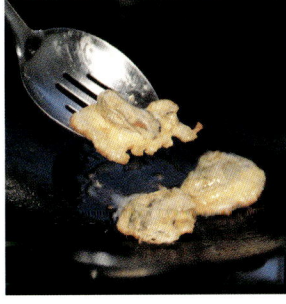

When cooked, remove from hot oil and drain with a perforated ladle.

Method

- Clean oysters in brine and rinse in clean water twice.
- Mix self-raising flour, plain flour and eggs together. Add water, pepper and salt. Blend well to form a smooth batter.
- Add oysters to batter. Drop 1 Tbsp of this mixture at a time into a wok of hot oil, over high heat. Fry until golden brown. Remove with a perforated ladle.
- Garnish with small sprigs of parsley. Serve with tomato sauce.

BRAISED FISH WITH BLACK BEAN SAUCE

Deep-fried whole fish braised in a light anchovy stock-based sauce.

Ingredients

Whole fish (garoupa, threadfin, red snapper)	1 kg (2 lb 3 oz)
Oil	for deep-frying
Shallots	2, peeled and sliced
Garlic	2 cloves, peeled and minced
Ginger	5 slices, peeled and minced
Fermented black beans	1 Tbsp, soaked in water for 10 minutes, drained and minced
Red chillies	2, chopped
Corn flour (cornstarch)	2 tsp, mixed with 2 Tbsp water
Spring onions (scallions)	2, chopped

Seasoning Ingredients

Salt	$1/2$ tsp
Pepper	$1/2$ tsp
Light soy sauce	2 tsp
Chinese rice wine	1 Tbsp
Egg white	1, beaten
Corn flour (cornstarch)	1 Tbsp, to be added just before frying fish

Sauce Ingredients (combined)

Fresh anchovy stock	250 ml (1 cup)
Light soy sauce	2 tsp
Thick soy sauce	$1/2$ tsp
Chinese rice wine	2 tsp
Black vinegar	1 tsp
Sugar	$1 1/2$ tsp
Salt	$1/4$ tsp
Pepper	$1/4$ tsp

STEP-BY-STEP

Coat whole fish with corn flour just before deep-frying.

Add chillies and sauce ingredients to stir-fried black beans, shallots, garlic and ginger.

Lower deep-fried fish gently into the wok. Reduce the heat a little and cover, allowing it to simmer until cooked.

Method

- Clean and scale fish. Cut two deep slits 2.25 cm (1 in) apart across each side of the body. Season fish with seasoning ingredients for at least 30 minutes. Just before deep-frying fish, coat with corn flour.
- Heat oil in a wok for deep-frying until hot. Fry fish for 2–3 minutes on each side. Remove and drain from oil.

- Reheat a clean wok with 2 Tbsp of the oil and stir-fry shallots, garlic and ginger until fragrant. Add fermented black beans and stir-fry until aromatic. Put in chillies and sauce ingredients.
- Return fish to the wok and reduce heat a little. Cover the wok and allow to simmer for 3–5 minutes, or until fish is cooked. Remove fish carefully and place on a serving dish.

- Thicken sauce with corn flour mixture and add spring onions. Pour sauce over fish and serve hot.

Add fish head pieces to batter and turn to coat completely. Deep-fry fish head pieces in hot oil until golden brown.

Heat up 3 Tbsp oil in the claypot. Add ginger and onion and sauté until fragrant.

Add fish head pieces to claypot. Then add bean curd cubes and cover to simmer for 5–8 minutes.

CLAYPOT FISH HEAD

Crunchy fish head served with a sweet and tangy sauce in a claypot.

Ingredients

Fish head (garoupa, threadfin, red snapper)	1, about 800 g (1¾ lb), chopped into large pieces
Chinese rice wine	½ Tbsp
Light soy sauce	½ Tbsp
Ginger juice	½ Tbsp
Pepper	½ tsp
Oil	for deep-frying
Soft bean curd	1 square piece, cut into 2.5-cm (1-in) cubes
Cooking oil	3 Tbsp
Ginger	2.5-cm (1-in) knob, peeled and sliced
Onion	1, cut into 6 wedges
Dried Chinese mushrooms	4
Canned button mushrooms	6–8
Red chillies	2, sliced
Spring onions (scallions)	2, cut into 2.5-cm (1 in) sections
Corn flour (cornstarch)	½ Tbsp, mixed with 1 Tbsp water
Lettuce leaves	6–8, washed

Batter

Egg	1, beaten
Corn flour (cornstarch)	2 Tbsp
Water	2 Tbsp

Sauce Ingredients

Chicken stock	250 ml (1 cup)
Oyster sauce	1 Tbsp
Light soy sauce	½ Tbsp
Chinese rice wine	2 tsp
Sesame oil	1 tsp
Sugar	1 tsp
Pepper	½ tsp

Method

- Clean fish head and marinate with rice wine, soy sauce, ginger juice and pepper for 30 minutes.
- Heat wok with oil for deep-frying until hot. Coat fish head with batter and deep-fry fish head for 5–8 minutes on each side until golden brown and cooked. Set aside.
- Put in bean curd and deep-fry for 2 minutes. Drain from oil and leave aside.
- Heat claypot with 3 Tbsp cooking oil and sauté ginger and onion until fragrant.
- Put in mushrooms and stir-fry for 1 minute. Add button mushrooms and chillies and toss briskly.
- Pour in combined sauce ingredients and bring to the boil.
- Put in fish head and bean curd. Reduce heat a little, cover and simmer for 5–8 minutes. Add spring onions and thicken with corn flour mixture.
- Arrange lettuce leaves around sides of claypot and serve immediately.

After mixing beef with flour, pepper and salt, shape into balls and flatten into patties.

Fry patties in a frying pan, turning over to cook both sides.

Add tomato quarters into frying pan after adding sugar.

S
T
E
P
-
B
Y
-
S
T
E
P

BEEF PATTIES IN TOMATO SAUCE

Tasty beef patties shallow-fried and cooked in tomato sauce.

Ingredients

Minced beef	450 g (1 lb)
Green (mung) bean flour	2 Tbsp
Pepper	a pinch
Salt	1/2 tsp
Cooking oil	6 Tbsp
Light soy sauce	1 Tbsp
Water	425 ml (1 3/4 cup)
Tomato sauce	2 Tbsp
Sugar	a pinch
Tomatoes	5, quartered
Worcestershire sauce	1/2 Tbsp

Method

- Mix beef with flour, pepper and salt. Shape into patties. Fry patties in oil over medium heat until golden brown. This will take about 5 minutes.
- Add soy sauce, water and tomato sauce. Simmer for 30 minutes over very low heat. Add sugar and tomatoes. Add Worcestershire sauce just before serving.

CHICKEN STEW WITH FRESH CHESTNUTS

Chunky chicken pieces stewed in rice wine with mushrooms and fresh chestnuts.

Ingredients

Chicken	1, about 1.75 kg (3 lb 13 1/2 oz)
Light soy sauce	1/2 tsp
Chestnuts	675 g (1 lb 6 1/2 oz)
Garlic	6 cloves
Preserved soy beans	2 Tbsp
Dried Chinese mushrooms	6
Oil	4 Tbsp
Rice wine	1 1/2 Tbsp
Water	800 ml (3 1/2 cups)
Brown sugar	a pinch
Salt	1/2 tsp
Green (mung) bean flour	1 Tbsp

S
T
E
P
-
B
Y
-
S
T
E
P

After treating chestnuts with hot and cold water, it will be easier to shell them and to remove the membrane inside.

Place peeled garlic and preserved soy beans in a mortar and pound to a paste.

After chopping up chicken, arrange pieces on a serving plate to form the shape of a whole chicken.

Method

- Rub chicken with soy sauce. Dip chestnuts in boiling water for 2 seconds, remove and leave in cold water for 3 minutes. Shell and remove hairy membrane. Peel garlic and pound to a paste with preserved soy beans. Soak mushrooms in water to soften. Discard stems and cut into big pieces.

- Fry pounded garlic and soy bean mixture in hot oil over medium heat for 3 minutes. Add chicken and turn briskly several times. Increase heat to brown chicken. Add rice wine, water, chestnuts, mushrooms, brown sugar and salt. Cover tightly and bring to the boil. Reduce heat and stew for 1 hour.

- Remove chicken to a chopping board and cut into large pieces. Arrange pieces on a plate in the form of a chicken. Add flour mixed to a paste with water to thicken gravy. Bring to the boil. Pour hot gravy over chicken. Place chestnuts around chicken and mushrooms on top.

FRIED GARLIC PORK

Thin slices of pork stir-fried in hot chilli and garlic sauce.

Ingredients

Pork fillet or tender cut	500 g (1 lb 1½ oz), thinly sliced
Oil	for deep-frying
Chilli oil	1 Tbsp
Garlic	10–12 cloves, peeled and sliced
Coriander (cilantro) leaves	2 sprigs for garnishing

Seasoning Ingredients

Light soy sauce	½ Tbsp
Five-spice powder	a pinch
Black peppercorns	1 tsp, lightly crushed
Corn flour (cornstarch)	2 tsp
Cooking oil	1 Tbsp, to be added just before cooking

Sauce Ingredients (combined)

Light soy sauce	½ Tbsp
Oyster sauce	1 tsp
Thick soy sauce	½ tsp
Sugar	½ tsp

S T E P - B Y - S T E P

Place seasoning ingredients in a mixing bowl and add pork to marinate for 30 minutes.

Add pork pieces to hot oil to deep-fry and stir lightly with a pair of long chopsticks to separate the pieces.

Stir-fry fried pork pieces in the combined sauce ingredients until sauce is quite dry.

Method

- Marinate pork with seasoning ingredients for 30 minutes. Just before cooking pork, stir in 1 Tbsp oil to prevent sticking.
- Heat oil for deep-frying until hot. Put in pork pieces, stirring lightly for 1 minute to separate meat. Drain well and set aside.
- Remove oil and add chilli oil. Heat until hot and lightly brown garlic.
- Pour in combined sauce ingredients then add fried pork and stir-fry for 2 minutes until sauce is quite dry.
- Dish onto a serving plate and garnish with coriander leaves.

Combine flour coating mixture ingredients in a mixing bowl. Place chicken pieces in mixture and turn to coat completely.

Dip chicken pieces into batter and deep-fry in hot oil until golden.

Scoop out chicken pieces and drain well with a perforated ladle.

FIVE-SPICE CRISPY SKIN CHICKEN

Crispy conflake-coated chicken served with lettuce and cucumber.

Ingredients

Chicken	1 kg (2 lb 3 oz) or 4 chicken thighs, cut into large pieces
Oil	for deep-frying
Lettuce and cucumber slices	

Seasoning

Sugar	1 Tbsp
Salt	1 tsp
Pepper	1 tsp
Five-spice powder	1/2 tsp
Egg	1, lightly beaten
Water	2 Tbsp
Self-raising flour	2 Tbsp

Flour Coating Mixture (combined)

Cornflakes	60 g (2 oz), finely ground
Self-raising flour	240 g (8 oz)
Salt	1/2 tsp
Pepper	1/2 tsp
Bicarbonate of soda	1/4 tsp

Batter

Self-raising flour	60 g (2 oz)
Water or milk	185 ml (3/4 cup)
Salt	1/4 tsp
Pepper	1/4 tsp

Method

- Marinate chicken pieces with seasoning ingredients for 1–2 hours.
- Just before frying, coat chicken pieces with flour coating mixture. Dip into batter mixture and drop into hot oil. Fry over high heat for 1 minute, then reduce heat to moderate and cook until chicken is golden in colour.
- Drain well and serve with lettuce or cucumber slices.

Scald trotters in boiling water for 5 minutes and drain well with a perforated ladle.

Stir-fry ground ingredients in a claypot until fragrant.

Pour in vinegar, sugar and enough water to cover all of the trotters.

PIG'S TROTTERS IN CHINESE BLACK VINEGAR

A delicious dish of fried pig's trotters simmered in black vinegar.

Ingredients

Pig's trotters	2, cleaned and cut into 5-cm (2-in) pieces
Cooking oil	3 Tbsp
Soy bean paste	5 dsp, ground
Chinese black vinegar	5 dsp
Sugar	2 tsp
Water	1.5 litres (6 cups) or enough to cover trotters
Thick soy sauce	1 tsp

Ground Ingredients

Shallots	15, peeled
Garlic	15 cloves, peeled
Red chillies	6

Method

- Boil a large saucepan of water and scald trotters for 5 minutes. Drain.
- Heat a saucepan or a deep claypot with oil until hot and stir-fry ground ingredients until fragrant. Add ground soy bean paste and continue to stir-fry until aromatic. Put in trotters and fry for another 3 minutes. If necessary, sprinkle with a little water to prevent burning. Add vinegar, sugar and enough water to cover trotters.
- Cover the pot and bring to the boil. Reduce heat and allow to simmer for 1 1/2 hours until trotters are tender, stirring occasionally to prevent sticking. When the trotters are tender, stir in thick soy sauce.

GINGER CHICKEN IN EARTHEN POT

Bite-sized chicken pieces cooked with mushrooms, carrots and bamboo shoots in a claypot.

Ingredients

Chicken	1, about 1 kg (2 lb 3 oz), cut into bite-sized pieces
Oil	for deep-frying
Firm bean curd	4 small squares, sliced into 1 x 2.5-cm (1/2 x 1-in) pieces
Cooking oil	2 Tbsp
Ginger	6 slices, peeled
Garlic	4 cloves, peeled and sliced
Shallots	4, peeled and sliced
Dried Chinese mushrooms	5, soaked until soft and halved
Carrots	120 g (4 oz), peeled and sliced
Canned bamboo shoots	90 g (3 oz), sliced
Tientsin cabbage	240 g (8 oz), cut into 5-cm (2-in) lengths
Red chillies	2, sliced
Spring onions (scallions)	6, cut into 2.5-cm (1-in) lengths

Seasoning Ingredients

Salt	1 tsp
Sugar	1 tsp
Thick soy sauce	1 tsp
Light soy sauce	2 tsp
Corn flour (cornstarch)	1 Tbsp

Sauce Ingredients (combined)

Fresh chicken stock	375 ml (1 1/2 cup)
Salt	1/2 tsp
Sugar	1 tsp
Pepper	1/2 tsp
Light soy sauce	1 Tbsp
Oyster sauce	1 Tbsp
Thick soy sauce	1 tsp
Sesame oil	1 tsp

S T E P - B Y - S T E P

Peel ginger and wipe it clean with a damp cloth. Cut into slices.

Place bean curd slices into oil one by one to prevent them from sticking to one another.

Add vegetables to the claypot and stir lightly to ensure that the ingredients are well mixed.

Method

- Marinate chicken with seasoning ingredients for 20 minutes.
- Heat oil in a wok until hot and deep-fry bean curd pieces until golden brown. Remove and set aside. Deep-fry chicken for 5 minutes. Drain and place in an earthen pot.
- Reheat a clean wok with 2 Tbsp of oil and lightly brown ginger, garlic and shallots. Put in mushrooms and stir-fry until fragrant. Add carrots, bamboo shoots and *Tientsin* cabbage and fry for 3–5 minutes. Put in sauce ingredients and bring to the boil.
- Pour over chicken in clay pot, add chillies and when it boils again, reduce heat, cover and simmer for 25 minutes or until chicken is tender.
- Add bean curd pieces and spring onions and simmer for another 5–10 minutes.
- Thicken sauce with corn flour mixture and serve.

TEOCHEW DUCK

Deep-fried duck simmered in light soy sauce and served with hard-boiled eggs.

Ingredients

Duck	1, clean weight about 1.5 kg
Salt	1 dsp
Five-spice powder	1 dsp
Galangal	120 g (4 oz), peeled and sliced
Oil	for deep-frying
Sugar	2 Tbsp
Thick soy sauce	2 Tbsp
Water	1.25 litres (5 cups) or enough to cover more than half the duck
Light soy sauce	1 Tbsp
Hard-boiled eggs	6, shelled
Coriander (cilantro) leaves	for garnishing

STEP-BY-STEP

Place duck on a flat surface. Rub duck all over, including the inside, with salt and five-spice powder.

Using a pair of tongs, fry duck in hot oil until lightly browned.

With a sharp knife, cut duck into slices for serving.

Method

- Rub inside and outside of duck with salt and five-spice powder. Stuff duck with the galangal slices, keeping 3 slices aside. Let duck stand for at least 2 hours.
- Heat deep-frying oil in a deep wok until hot and fry duck for 5 minutes until lightly browned. Remove duck and drain well. Pour off oil, leaving 2 Tbsp in the wok and add sugar and 3 galangal slices. When the oil turns dark golden, turn off heat. Add thick soy sauce. Return duck to wok and coat the whole duck with sauce.
- Pour in water to cover more than half of the duck. Put in light soy sauce and hard-boiled eggs. Bring to the boil, cover and simmer for about 20 minutes. Remove eggs and set aside.
- Turn duck and continue simmering over low heat for about 1 1/2–2 hours, until duck is tender and sauce is thick. Turn duck occasionally while simmering.
- Before serving, cut duck into serving size pieces and halve eggs. Place around duck and pour sauce over. Serve garnished with coriander leaves.

When ribs are roasting on the wire rack, baste them with marinade occasionally and turn them over every 15 minutes.

Add maltose to the remaining portion of marinade and cook over low heat.

Dip ribs into maltose mixture to coat completely. Then grill until well roasted.

ROAST PORK RIBS

Pork ribs marinated in garlic and ginger and roasted over a slow fire.

Ingredients

Pork ribs	1.2 kg (2 lb 12 oz), kept in whole panels about 10–12-cm (4–5-in) long
Garlic	4 cloves, peeled and finely chopped
Ginger	2 thin slices, peeled
Star anise	1 piece
Maltose	1 Tbsp

Seasoning Ingredients

Coarse sugar	120 g (4 oz)
Light soy sauce	3 Tbsp
Thick soy sauce	1 tsp
Oyster sauce	2 Tbsp
Hoisin sauce	1½ Tbsp
Plum sauce	1½ Tbsp
Chinese rice wine	1 Tbsp
Ginger powder	½ tsp
Five-spice powder	1 tsp
Sesame oil	1 Tbsp
Pepper	¼ tsp
Meat tenderizer	2 tsp
Red colouring	¼ tsp

Method

- Rinse panels of ribs. Dry well with kitchen paper.
- Mix seasoning ingredients in a bowl. Put in garlic, ginger and star anise. Mix well. Pour mixture over ribs and marinate for at least 8–10 hours (preferably overnight) in the refrigerator.
- Preheat oven to 220°C (440°F) for 15 minutes. Place ribs on a wire rack and roast for at least 1 hour, basting ribs with marinade occasionally and turning ribs over every 15 minutes.
- Pour remaining marinade into a small saucepan and add maltose. Stir over low heat until maltose dissolves.
- To coat ribs, dip them one by one into maltose mixture. Grill on each side for 3–5 minutes, or until well roasted.

Stir-fried Prawns with Cloud Ear Fungus and Snow Peas

Stir-fried Sweet and Sour Cabbage

Braised Dried Bean Curd with Dried Chinese Mushrooms

Bean Sprouts and Carrot with Salted Fish

Stir-fried Aubergines with Minced Meat

Make a small slit on the back of the prawn. Use a paring knife to remove black vein.

Stir-fry ingredients quickly to heat them through.

Remove from heat once sauce bubbles to avoid overcooking prawns.

STIR-FRIED PRAWNS WITH CLOUD EAR FUNGUS AND SNOW PEAS

Medium-sized prawns stir-fried with cloud ear fungus and snow peas in chicken stock and light soy sauce.

Ingredients

Prawns (shrimps)	250 g (9 oz), medium-sized, peeled and deveined
Oil	for deep-frying
Cooking oil	2 Tbsp
Snow peas	150 g (5 oz), cleaned
Garlic	2 cloves, peeled and finely chopped
Young ginger	2-cm (1-in) knob, peeled and finely chopped
Cloud ear fungus (*wan yee*)	10 large pieces, soaked to soften

Seasoning Ingredients

Salt	1 tsp
Sugar	1/2 tsp
Egg white	1/2, beaten

Sauce Ingredients (combined)

Chicken stock	180 ml (3/4 cup)
Light soy sauce	1 Tbsp
Oyster sauce	1/2 Tbsp
Chinese rice wine	1/2 Tbsp
Corn flour (cornstarch)	2 tsp

Method

- Marinate prawns with seasoning ingredients for 30 minutes. Heat oil for deep-frying in a saucepan and blanch prawns in hot oil for 10 seconds. Drain and set aside.
- Heat a wok with 2 Tbsp cooking oil and stir-fry snow peas for 15 seconds. Drain and set aside.
- Put in garlic and ginger to brown. Add cloud ear fungus and prawns. Toss well.
- Pour in combined sauce ingredients and bring to the boil. Return snow peas and mix well before transferring to serving dish.

STIR-FRIED SWEET AND SOUR CABBAGE

A simple stir-fry of cabbage with chilli and peanut oil.

Ingredients

Chinese celery cabbage (Chinese leaves)	700–900 g (1½ lb–1 lb 15½ oz)
Rice or wine vinegar	4–6 tsp
Sugar	4–6 tsp
Light soy sauce	4–6 tsp
Salt	a large pinch
Tapioca or potato flour	1–1½ tsp
Peanut (groundnut) or corn oil	4–5 Tbsp
Chillies	1 large or 2 small, seeded and cut into thread-like strips
Sesame oil	2–3 tsp for sprinkling

STEP-BY-STEP

Cut Chinese celery cabbage into half lengthways then slice into 5-cm strips.

Drain cabbage in a sieve. In the meantime, wipe the wok dry and carry on with the next step.

When sauce starts to bubble, add drained cabbage to the wok. Stir well so that cabbage will absorb sauce.

Method

- Remove any tough leaves from Chinese celery cabbage, halve the rest lengthways and slice across into 5-cm (2-in) strips. Mix the vinegar, sugar, soy sauce, salt and tapioca or potato flour. Reserve.

- Heat a wok until hot. Add 2–3 Tbsp of groundnut or corn oil and swirl it around. Add cabbage. Going to the bottom of the wok with a spatula, stir and toss cabbage continuously for 5–6 minutes. If the pieces begin to burn, lower heat. The cabbage bulk will decrease. Transfer cabbage to a colander and drain.

- Wipe the wok dry and reheat it. Add the rest of the oil, swirl it around, then add chilli strips, stirring twice, and then add sauce. When sauce bubbles, add cabbage.
- Stir and toss to let cabbage absorb sauce. When thoroughly hot, transfer to a warmed serving dish. Sprinkle sesame oil over cabbage and serve immediately.

BRAISED DRIED BEAN CURD WITH DRIED CHINESE MUSHROOMS

Dried mushrooms and broccoli add a distinctive flavour to this unique bean curd dish.

Ingredients

Dried Chinese mushrooms	8–10, soaked until soft
Cooking oil	3 Tbsp
Ginger	2 slices, peeled and shredded
Shallot	1, peeled and sliced
Broccoli	90 g (3 oz), cut into small florets and rinsed
Dried bean curd cubes	250 g (9 oz)
Corn flour (cornstarch)	1 tsp, mixed with 1 Tbsp chicken stock or water
Sesame oil	1 tsp
Red chilli	1, sliced (optional)
Spring onion (scallion)	1, chopped

Seasoning Ingredients

Salt	$\frac{1}{4}$ tsp
Sugar	$\frac{1}{4}$ tsp
Pepper	$\frac{1}{4}$ tsp
Light soy sauce	1 tsp

Sauce Ingredients (combined)

Fresh chicken stock	300 ml ($1\frac{1}{4}$ cup)
Thick soy sauce	$\frac{1}{2}$ Tbsp
Light soy sauce	2 tsp
Sugar	$\frac{1}{2}$ tsp
Salt	$\frac{1}{4}$ tsp
Pepper	$\frac{1}{4}$ tsp

STEP-BY-STEP

Use a paring knife to cut broccoli into small florets.

Add mushrooms to stir-fried ginger and shallots. Fry for a further 1–2 minutes.

Fry bean curd cubes in the wok, turning round until all sides are light brown in colour.

Method

- Season mushrooms with seasoning ingredients for 15 minutes.
- Heat $1\frac{1}{2}$ Tbsp of oil in a wok until hot and stir-fry ginger and shallots until fragrant, then add mushrooms and fry for another 1–2 minutes. Remove and set aside. Stir-fry broccoli for 1 minute, remove and set aside.
- Reheat remaining oil in the wok and toss bean curd cubes until crisp and light brown in colour.
- Add combined sauce ingredients and mushrooms and bring to the boil. Reduce heat and simmer for 10 minutes. Add broccoli and simmer for 2 minutes longer.
- Thicken with corn flour mixture and lastly sprinkle in sesame oil, red chillies and spring onion.

Peel small carrot. Cut into thin shreds.

Remove salted fish from water and drain. Use a cleaver to cut it into thin slices.

Add bean sprouts and carrot to the same wok and stir-fry for about 2 minutes.

S
T
E
P
-
B
Y
-
S
T
E
P

BEAN SPROUTS AND CARROT WITH SALTED FISH

Crispy bean sprouts stir-fried with shredded carrots and topped with salted fish.

Ingredients

Salted fish	1 piece, about 5-cm (2-in) square
Oil	4 Tbsp
Garlic	1 clove, peeled and chopped
Bean sprouts	450 g (1 lb)
Small carrot	1, peeled and shredded
Light soy sauce	$1/2$ Tbsp

Method

- Soak salted fish in water for a few minutes, then drain and slice thinly.
- Heat oil in a wok. Brown garlic, then add salted fish. Fry until fragrant, then scoop out to a dish.
- Use the same oil to stir-fry bean sprouts and shredded carrot for about 2 minutes. Season with light soy sauce.
- Garnish with salted fish and serve immediately before bean sprouts go limp.

Drain aubergines and add to the wok. Turn up heat to stir-fry aubergines until soft.

Reheat wok and add in ginger, garlic and hot bean paste. Continue stir-frying until fragrant.

Pour chicken stock into wok. When stock starts to boil, return aubergines to wok and stir well to combine.

STEP-BY-STEP

STIR-FRIED AUBERGINES WITH MINCED MEAT

Aubergines fried with minced meat and hot bean paste served with spring onions and coriander leaves

Ingredients

Aubergines (eggplants/brinjal)	3, medium, cut into 5 x 1.25-cm 2 x $^{3}/_{4}$ in) pieces
Cooking oil	4 Tbsp
Garlic	4 cloves, peeled and minced
Ginger	3 slices, peeled
Garlic	2 cloves, peeled
Hot bean paste	$^{1}/_{2}$ Tbsp
Lean pork with a little fat or chicken	120 g (4 oz), coarsely minced
Fresh chicken stock	125 ml ($^{1}/_{2}$ cup)
Corn flour (cornstarch)	$^{1}/_{2}$ Tbsp, mixed with 1 Tbsp water
Spring onions (scallions)	2, chopped
Coriander (cilantro) leaves	1 sprig, chopped

Sauce Ingredients (combined)

Light soy sauce	1 Tbsp
Pepper	$^{1}/_{4}$ tsp
Salt	$^{1}/_{4}$ tsp
Sugar	$^{1}/_{2}$ tsp
Sesame oil	1 tsp

Method

- Soak cut aubergines in a little salt water.
- Heat wok until hot with 3 Tbsp of cooking oil. Reduce heat a little to lightly brown garlic. Put in drained aubergines and stir-fry over high heat until soft. Remove and leave aside.

- Reheat wok with 1 Tbsp cooking oil. Stir-fry ginger, garlic and hot bean paste until aromatic. Put in minced meat and when it changes colour, add combined sauce ingredients and stir-fry for 2 minutes.

- Pour in chicken stock and when it begins to boil, return pre-fried aubergines to the wok and stir to mix well.
- Thicken with corn flour mixture. Sprinkle in spring onions and coriander leaves, and transfer to serving dish.

Place prawns in a mixing bowl and marinate well with salt, sugar, pepper and sesame oil.

After shallots are browned, add noodles to the wok and stir-fry for 1–2 minutes.

Pour combined sauce ingredients into the wok. Stir to mix well. Add in fried meat mixture and combine with noodles.

FRIED YELLOW NOODLES WITH MEAT AND PRAWNS

A complete meal of yellow noodles, meat and prawns in a light gravy.

Ingredients

Small prawns (shrimps)	120 g (4 oz), shelled, deveined and washed
Salt	1/4 tsp
Sugar	1/4 tsp
Dash of pepper and sesame oil	
Chicken or pork meat	120 g (4 oz), shredded
Light soy sauce	1/4 tsp
Sugar	1/4 tsp
Corn flour (cornstarch)	1/2 tsp
Cooking oil	3 Tbsp
Garlic	2 cloves, peeled and minced
Mustard green (choy sum)	2 stalks, washed and cut into 5-cm (2-in) lengths
Shallots	4, peeled and sliced
Fresh yellow noodles	300 g (10 oz)
Corn flour (cornstarch)	1 tsp, mixed with 1 Tbsp water
Crisp-fried shallots	1 Tbsp
Spring onion (scallion)	1, chopped

Sauce Ingredients (combined)

Fresh chicken or pork bone stock	125 ml (1/2 cup)
Light soy sauce	1 Tbsp
Thick soy sauce	1/2 tsp
Sugar	1/2 tsp
Salt	1/4 tsp
Pepper	1/4 tsp

Method

- Marinate prawns with salt, sugar, pepper and sesame oil and meat with light soy sauce, sugar and corn flour and leave for 15 minutes.
- Heat 1 Tbsp oil in a wok until hot and lightly brown garlic. Put in meat, then prawns and toss until meat changes colour. Add mustard green and stir-fry for 1 minute. Remove and leave aside.

- Reheat wok with 2 Tbsp oil and lightly brown shallots. Put in noodles and stir-fry briskly for 1-2 minutes.
- Stir in combined sauce ingredients and return fried meat mixture to the wok. Stir well and thicken with corn flour mixture. Garnish with crisp-fried shallots and spring onion.

FRIED FLAT RICE NOODLES WITH BEEF

Beef marinated in ginger juice and corn flour add colour and taste to fried flat rice noodles.

Ingredients

Beef	120 g (4 oz), cut into thin slices
Cooking oil	6 Tbsp
Salt	1/2 tsp
Mustard green	5 small stalks, both ends trimmed
Fresh flat rice noodles separate strands	300 g (10 oz), loosened with fingers to
Light soy sauce	1 Tbsp, mixed with 1 Tbsp chicken stock or water
Bean sprouts	100 g, tailed
Spring onion (scallion)	1, cut into 2.5-cm (1-in) lengths
Coriander (cilantro) leaves	1 sprig, cut into 2.5-cm (1-in) lengths

Seasoning Ingredients

Bicarbonate of soda	1/3 tsp
Ginger juice	1 dsp
Salt	1/2 tsp
Sugar	1/4 tsp
Corn flour (cornstarch)	2 tsp
Cooking oil	1 Tbsp, added after all the above ingredients are well mixed with the meat

Sauce Ingredients (combined)

Fresh chicken stock	5 Tbsp
Light soy sauce	1/2 tsp
Thick soy sauce	2 tsp
Corn flour (cornstarch)	3 tsp

S T E P - B Y - S T E P

Using a pair of kitchen scissors, snip away both ends of mustard greens.

Scald mustard green very quickly then drain well.

When meat mixture is cooked, pour on top of noodles.

Method

- Marinate beef with seasoning ingredients for at least 20 minutes.
- Bring half a saucepan of water to the boil. Add 1 Tbsp oil and 1/2 tsp salt. Scald mustard green until just cooked. Drain well and arrange on an oval dish. Turn off heat and scald beef. Allow to soak for 1 minute. Remove scum from surface, then drain meat and leave aside.
- Heat wok with 1 Tbsp of oil. Ensure that the whole wok is well greased, then pour off excess oil. Put in rice noodles and toss in hot wok for 2 minutes.
- Add light soy sauce mixed with chicken stock, and stir-fry until well mixed. Remove and place noodles on mustard green.

- Reheat wok with 1 Tbsp of oil and stir-fry bean sprouts for 30 seconds. Remove and place over fried rice noodles.
- Wash wok and reheat with 1 Tbsp of oil. Put in combined sauce ingredients. Add meat, then spring onion and coriander leaves. Toss quickly then add 2 Tbsp of cooking oil and mix.
- Pour meat mixture over noodles. Serve with cut red chillies and light soy sauce.

RICE PORRIDGE

Soft-boiled rice served with pork, liver and fish slices.

Ingredients

Fish fillet (any kind)	450 g (1 lb), thinly sliced
Pork	90 g (3 oz), thinly sliced
Liver	60 g (2 oz), thinly sliced
Ginger juice	2 tsp
Rice wine	1 tsp
Light soy sauce	1 Tbsp
Long grain rice	225 g (8 oz)
Minced pork	120 g (4 oz)
Salt	to taste
Lard	1 Tbsp
Pepper	
Parsley	2 sprigs, chopped
Crisp-fried shallots	1 Tbsp

S
T
E
P
-
B
Y
-
S
T
E
P

Place rice in a pot and fill with adequate water to wash.

Add pork slices and stir into porridge.

Break a raw egg into the rice bowl then scoop boiling porridge over.

Method

- Season fish fillet, sliced pork and liver with ginger juice, rice wine, and soy sauce.
- Wash rice and boil in 1.5 litres (6 cups) water over medium heat for 30 minutes. Add minced pork, stir to mix well and boil over low heat for another 90 minutes. Add salt.
- When rice is still boiling, add seasoned ingredients. Turn off heat immediately. Stir in lard. Serve in individual bowls, garnished with pepper, chopped parsley and crisp-fried shallots. If desired, a raw egg may be broken into each bowl before boiling porridge is ladled in.

Stir and toss prawns with a wooden spatula until they turn pinkish.

Using a cleaver, chop spring onions into thin rounds. Sort out white and green rounds into separate parts.

When frying rice, use a wooden spatula to turn and toss rice, starting from the bottom of the wok.

FRIED RICE

Stir-fried rice with prawns, ham and peas garnished with egg strips.

Ingredients

Cooked rice	600 g (1 lb 5 oz)
Prawns (shrimps)	225 g (8 oz), shelled and deveined
Cooking oil	8 Tbsp
Garlic	2 cloves, peeled and finely chopped
Shao Hsing wine or medium-dry sherry	1 Tbsp
Salt	
Freshly ground black pepper	
Spring onions (scallions)	4
Eggs	2, large
Peas	225 g (8 oz)
Cooked ham	225 g (8 oz), diced
Dark soy sauce	1$\frac{1}{2}$ Tbsp
Chicken stock	2–3 Tbsp
Thick soy sauce	1 tsp (optional)
Marinade	
Salt	$\frac{1}{2}$ tsp
Corn flour (cornstarch)	2$\frac{1}{2}$ tsp
Egg white	1 Tbsp

Method

- Cut prawns into 2-cm (1-in) pieces.
- Mix marinade ingredients and stir in prawns. Coat evenly and refrigerate.
- Heat a wok over high heat until it smokes. Add 2 Tbsp oil and swirl it around. Add in chopped garlic and when it browns, add prawns. When prawns turn pinkish, add wine or sherry along the rim of the wok. As soon as the sizzling dies down, remove prawns and reserve them. Wash and dry the wok.
- Chop spring onions across into rounds, separating the greens from the whites.
- Beat eggs lightly with 1 Tbsp of the oil and a little salt. Heat a large flat frying pan until moderately hot, add 1 Tbsp oil and swirl it around to cover the whole surface.
- Pour in half the beaten egg and tip the pan to spread egg evenly to the edges. When firm, turn egg over and fry the other side for a few seconds. Put egg on a plate and slice into strips.
- Stir cooked rice to loosen it. Blanch peas in boiling water for 3 minutes and drain.
- Reheat the wok over high heat until it smokes. Add remaining oil and swirl it around. Add white rounds of spring onion and stir.
- Pour in remaining egg and tip in the rice. Toss rice, separating any lumps.
- When rice is thoroughly hot, add ham, stir, peas, stir and prawns. Still stirring, add soy sauce and stock. Stir in the extra thick soy sauce for a more pronounced colour if desired. Finally, stir in half the egg strips and serve warm. Top with remaining egg strips and spring onions.

After soaking for 10 minutes, remove transparent noodles from water with a pair of chopsticks.

Heat up oil in a pot and stir-fry shallots and garlic to lightly brown them.

Add in fish balls to soup and boil for a further 2–3 minutes.

TRANSPARENT NOODLES AND FISH BALL SOUP

Transparent noodles adda different twist to this popular fish ball soup.

Ingredients

Transparent noodles	45 g (1½ oz), cut into 10-cm (4-in) lengths and soaked for 10 minutes
Cooking oil	2 Tbsp
Shallots	2, peeled and sliced
Garlic	2 cloves, peeled and minced
Fresh anchovy or chicken stock	1 litre (4 cups)
Preserved dried Chinese white cabbage (*tung choy*)	2 tsp, rinsed
Fish balls	15, medium, rinsed
Salt and pepper	
Spring onions (scallions)	2, chopped

Method

- Drain soft transparent noodles and set aside.
- Heat oil in a pot until hot and stir-fry shallots and garlic until lightly browned. Remove shallots and garlic crisps from oil and set aside.
- Pour in strained stock and bring to the boil. Add transparent noodles and preserved dried Chinese white cabbage and boil for 5 minutes. Put in the fish balls and boil for 2–3 minutes longer. Add salt and pepper to taste.
- Serve hot soup garnished with a sprinkling of shallot and garlic crisps and spring onions.

STEAMED CHICKEN GLUTINOUS RICE
(LOR MA KAI)

Chicken richly-flavoured in oyster sauce, ginger juice and sesame oil is steamed covered in glutinous rice.

Ingredients

Chicken	1.5 kg (3 lb 4$^{1}/_{2}$ oz)
Glutinous rice	1 kg (2 lb 3 oz)
Cooking oil	8 Tbsp
Dried Chinese mushrooms	60 g (2 oz), soaked and cut into strips
Shallots	8, peeled and sliced
Salt	2 tsp
Thick soy sauce	1 tsp
Five-spice powder	1 heaped tsp
Water	1 litre (4 cups)
Red chillies	2, seeded and sliced
Spring onions (scallions)	2, chopped
Coriander (cilantro) leaves	4 sprigs, cut into 2.5-cm (1-in) lengths
Chilli sauce	

Seasoning Ingredients

Oyster sauce	4 Tbsp
Rice wine	2 tsp
Thick soy sauce	1 tsp
Light soy sauce	2 tsp
Ginger juice	2 tsp
Sesame oil	1 tsp
Sugar	1 tsp
Pepper	$^{1}/_{2}$ tsp
Corn flour (cornstarch)	1 heaped tsp

Ease meat away from bone with a paring knife while holding bone with the other hand.

Press rice down after every spoonful to ensure that bowl is well-packed.

Be cautious when lifting the lid of the steamer to avoid scalding.

Method

- Debone chicken and cut into 1.5-cm ($^{3}/_{4}$-in) thick slices. Season with seasoning ingredients for at least 1 hour.
- Wash and drain glutinous rice and steam for 45 minutes.
- Heat oil in a wok and fry mushrooms for 1–2 minutes. Drain from oil and leave aside.
- Lightly brown shallots and put in glutinous rice, salt, thick soy sauce and five-spice powder and fry for 1 minute. Add water, mix well and simmer gently, covered, for 5–10 minutes. Remove from heat.
- Grease 12 medium rice bowls and put in some fried mushrooms and seasoned chicken at the bottom of each bowl. Fill with glutinous rice and press with the back of a spoon to fill half of rice bowl.
- Steam over rapidly boiling water for 45 minutes.
- To serve, turn steamed glutinous rice onto a small dish. Garnish with chillies, spring onions and coriander leaves and serve hot with chilli sauce.

PORK CHOW MIEN

Chinese noodles fried with pork, mushrooms and prawns served with shredded lettuce.

Ingredients

Chinese noodles or spaghetti	225 g (8 oz)
Prawns (shrimps)	100 g (3½ oz), large, boiled and peeled
Salt and freshly ground black pepper	
Vegetable oil	4 Tbsp
Onions	2 medium, peeled, halved and thinly sliced
Streaky pork	100 g (3½ oz), or leftover roast pork or lamb, cut into matchstick strips
Button mushrooms	3–4 large, cut into thick matchstick strips
Soy sauce	3½ Tbsp
Dry sherry	3 Tbsp
Butter or lard	2 Tbsp
Large lettuce leaves	3, shredded

Place noodles in a colander and run cold water through to prevent noodles from sticking.

After stir-frying the onion, add in pork and mushroom matchsticks and continue stir-frying.

Pour noodles into the wok and stir well to combine with the rest of the ingredients.

Method

- Boil noodles or spaghetti in salted water for 6–12 minutes or until just tender, then drain and rinse under cold water to separate the strands. Sprinkle prawns with salt and pepper to taste, and rub this seasoning in.
- Heat oil in a wok or large saucepan over high heat. Add onions and stir-fry for 1 minute. Add pork and mushroom matchsticks and stir-fry with onions for 1 minutes 30 seconds. Sprinkle over two-thirds of the soy sauce and stir-fry for another 1 minute 30 seconds. Turn the heat to medium.
- Add noodles or spaghetti to the pan and stir until all the ingredients are well mixed. Sprinkle in the rest of the soy sauce and half the sherry, reduce the heat and simmer for 2–3 minutes.
- Heat butter or lard in a small frying-pan over medium heat. When it starts melting, add prawns and stir-fry them for 1 minutes 30 seconds. Add lettuce and stir-fry for 30 seconds. Place mixture from the wok in a large, deep and well heated serving dish. Put prawns and lettuce on top and sprinkle with the remaining sherry to serve.

As rock sugar mixture is boiling, start to add in water chestnut cubes.

Pass flour mixture through a strainer to refine.

Drizzle egg white into soup and stir with a ladle at the same time.

S
T
E
P
-
B
Y
-
S
T
E
P

GINGKO NUT AND WATER CHESTNUT DESSERT

A sweet dessert made with gingko nuts and water chestnuts.

Ingredients

Water	1.5 litres (6 cups)
Rock sugar	300 g (10 oz)
Gingko nuts	180 g (6 oz), shelled and bitter centres removed
Water chestnuts	22, skinned and diced into 0.5-cm (1/4-in) cubes
Egg whites	2, lightly beaten
Sweet potato flour	3 Tbsp
Corn flour (cornstarch)	1 Tbsp
Water	125 ml (1/2 cup)

Method

- In a large saucepan, bring water and rock sugar to a slow boil. When rock sugar dissolves, put in gingko nuts. Boil over low heat for 10 minutes, then add water chestnuts. Simmer for another 10 minutes.
- Combine sweet potato flour, corn flour and water, and strain mixture.
- Slowly drizzle and stir egg white into soup. Repeat with flour solution. When it boils again, remove from heat.
- Serve hot or cold.

SWEET DUMPLINGS

Fried glutinous rice balls filled with delicious red bean paste

Ingredients

Glutinous rice flour	225 g (8 oz)
Canned red bean paste	225 g (8 oz)
Corn or vegetable oil	(optional)

STEP-BY-STEP

Press a small piece of dough into a round shape then press a thumb into the centre.

Place 1 tsp bean paste in the centre then cover dough over bean paste.

Using a slotted spoon, scoop out dumplings and drain them. Place dumplings onto a warmed serving plate.

Method

- Stir 225 ml ($^9/_{10}$ cup) cold water gradually into the flour and work it into a smooth dough. There is no need to knead.
- Take a small piece of dough about the size of a chestnut and shape it into a round. Press a thumb into the round.
- Insert 1 tsp bean paste and work dough over bean paste completely: Roll dumpling between the palms to make it round. Repeat until all the dough and bean paste are used.
- Bring 1.4 litres ($5^5/_8$ cups) of water to the boil in a large saucepan. Add about half of the dumplings, one by one, and let water come back to the boil. Move dumplings once or twice with a wooden spoon to prevent them from sticking to the pan.
- Reduce the heat but continue to boil for 5–6 minutes or until dough looks transparent.
- Lift out dumplings with a slotted spoon, drain them, and put them onto a warmed serving plate. Cook the rest of the dumplings in the same way, draining them thoroughly and putting them on the serving plate.
- Serve hot as they are or, if wished, when they are drained, fry them in a little oil over medium low heat, gently stirring, until they begin to brown; this gives the sticky dumplings a delicious crisp outer coating.
- Dumplings can be frozen after step 3. It takes 8–9 minutes to cook them from frozen in boiling water and, again, they can be fried if wished.

SWEET YAM PASTE (AU NEE)

A tasty dessert of mashed yam, boiled gingko nuts and pumpkin cubes.

Ingredients

Gingko nuts	115 g (4 oz), shelled
Sugar	227 g (8 oz)
Pumpkin	225 g (8 oz), diced into 2-cm (1-in) cubes
Yam	905 g (2 lb), diced into 5-cm x 1-cm (2 x ½ in) cubes
Castor sugar	12 Tbsp
Lard	6 Tbsp
Shallots	3, peeled and sliced thinly

S T E P - B Y - S T E P

Using a paring knife, cut gingko nuts into halves and remove the fibre within.

Mash half of the yam with oil and sugar. Continue mashing until texture is smooth.

After shallots are lightly browned, add in yam paste and stir-fry over low heat.

Method

- Wash gingko nuts. Boil with half of the sugar in 2 Tbsp water over low heat for 45 minutes until sugar is absorbed into nuts. Add water a little at a time while cooking. Cool and cut gingko nuts into half, removing centre fibre if any.
- Cook pumpkin cubes in remaining sugar and 2 Tbsp water over low heat in a heavy-bottomed saucepan. Cook until sugar is absorbed. Add a little water at a time while cooking to prevent sugar from burning. Set gingko nuts and pumpkins aside.
- Steam yam pieces over rapidly boiling water until very soft. Use a food processor to blend half of the yam, 2 Tbsp lard and half of the sugar until paste is smooth. Remove to a bowl and repeat with remaining yam, lard and remaining sugar.
- Heat another 2 Tbsp lard in a wok to fry sliced shallots until very lightly browned. Put in yam paste and stir-fry over low heat for 30 seconds. Remove to a shallow serving bowl. Place cooked pumpkin cubes around sides of the bowl and gingko nuts over the yam. Serve hot.

Place peanuts in a wok and roast until light brown.

Blend rice and half portion of the peanuts with 455 ml water in an electric blender. Process until very fine.

Bring mixture to the boil over moderate heat, making sure to stir continuously with a wooden spoon.

S T E P - B Y - S T E P

GROUNDNUT CRÈME

Blended groundnuts and rice boiled with sugar and water is a perfect dessert to end off a meal.

Ingredients

Peanuts (groundnuts)	625 g (1 lb 6 oz), shelled
Rice	2 Tbsp, washed and drained
Water	2 litres (8 cups)
Sugar	310 g (11 oz)

Method

- Roast peanuts until light brown. Remove skin.
- Using an electric blender, blend rice and half of the peanuts with 455 ml (1¾ cup) water until very fine. Add 2–3 Tbsp of water if necessary to keep the mixture moving and rotating. Pour into a bowl and set aside.
- Repeat process using the other half of the peanuts with another 455 ml water (1¾ cup).
- Place blended peanuts, sugar and remaining water in a heavy-bottomed aluminium saucepan. Bring to the boil over a moderate heat. Stir mixture all the time with a wooden spoon. Let simmer for 5 minutes, stirring continuously. Remove from heat. Serve hot or cold.

Glossary of Ingredients

Index

GLOSSARY & INDEX

GLOSSARY OF INGREDIENTS

Mushrooms (tung ku)

There are several different types of mushrooms used in Chinese cooking. They are champignons or button mushrooms (mou ku), straw mushrooms and dried Chinese mushrooms.

You can easily find fresh champignons or canned button mushrooms in supermarkets. Choose the white unblemished ones and when preparing, do not peel off the skin unless it is bruised. They usually cook in about 5 minutes and are good for combining with meats and other vegetables. They are also delicious when used in soups.

Straw mushrooms (tsin cho ku) have been named as such because they are cultivated in straw. You can buy them either fresh or canned, but fresh ones have to be scalded before use. After scalding, they can be only stored in the refrigerator for a few days.

There are two varieties of dried Chinese mushrooms, the winter mushroom (tung ku) and the flower mushroom (fah ku). The former is thick and greyish black in colour while the latter is paler in colour and more expensive. Before cooking, soak them in water for at least 30 minutes to soften.

Reserve the stems for flavouring stocks, especially for strict vegetarian cooking. Remove the stems, wash, dry and grind with a pepper mill or an electric blender until fine for the stock. To store for a long period of time, ensure that they are well dried before blending and store in the refrigerator in an air-tight container.

Bamboo shoots

Canned bamboo shoots are convenient to use but remember to rinse them thoroughly before use. If you are using fresh bamboo shoots, peel off the outer skin and cut away the tough fibrous layer. Then boil the shoots in slightly salted water with 1/2 Tbsp of sugar for about 30 minutes. Boil in fresh water for 15 minutes. Bamboo shoots can keep up to 2 weeks if properly frozen.

Broccoli

When choosing broccoli, pick the dark green ones with a firm and closely-packed head. The harder parts of the stems can be pared and then sliced for cooking. Before stir-frying broccoli, blanch it in boiling salted water with a little oil first to cook it slightly. Alternatively, you can toss it in a little hot oil for a minute or two.

Mustard green (choy sum)

Choy Sum is a green leafy vegetable with light green stems. It is suitable for frying with noodles because it is crunchy and juicy but it is equally tasty when fried on its own or made into a soup.

Mustard green is also used pickled to make salty pickled mustard green (harm mui choy) and slightly sweet pickled mustard green (tim mui choy). Both of these are partially dried. Before use, you need to wash carefully and constantly change the water to get rid of fine sand particles.

Dried mustard green (choy korn) is used to make soups. It has to be soaked until softened and washed carefully prior to

Coriander leaves (cilantro)

Coriander is also known as Chinese parsley. The leaves have a strong flavour and are usually used for flavouring and garnishing food. The flavour is different from English parsley so you should not use it as a substitute but it is acceptable as

Snow peas

Snow peas are flat pea pods and light green in colour. Before cooking, you have to wash and soak them in water to prevent the peas from splitting when cooked. After cooking, break the ends of the pod slightly to remove the fibre from the side edges of the pea pods.

White cabbage (pak choy)

The Chinese white cabbage is a long leaf cabbage with green leaves. It has a bland taste and is quite watery. There is also a shorter variety with light green stems called the Shanghai white cabbage (siew pak choy).

Celery

Look for crisp light green celery with young stalks when choosing. Avoid using very large stalks since they may be fibrous. The fibres will require removing before slicing the stalk into smaller pieces.

Galangal
Native to Southern China, galangal is from the same family as ginger but it cannot be used to substitute ginger. It is commonly used for making medicinal herbal mixtures and to cover up the strong flavour of meats like duck and lamb.

Ginger
The pungent ginger root is used to reduce the strong flavours in meat and the 'fishy' smells in fish. 2 types of ginger are used in Chinese cooking, young ginger and old ginger. Young ginger, as compared to old ginger, is juicier, less pungent and has a paler skin colour. Before using ginger, you have to peel off the skin by scraping it with a paring knife. Then cut it according to the recipe. If fresh ginger is unavailable, it is better to omit it than to use dried or powdered ginger as a substitute.

Garlic
Garlic is used in Chinese cooking to flavour oil, especially when stir-frying. Make sure that you only use fresh garlic. Garlic powder and flakes are inadequate substitutes for fresh garlic.

Szechuan vegetable (char choy)
The Szechuan vegetable is actually preserved Chinese radish pickled in salt and chillies. When you buy it, you can still see the chilli powder coating the olive green coloured vegetable. Before using it, you have to wash it carefully and leave it to soak in water to reduce its saltiness.

Chinese dates
Red dates are dark red in colour and have a sweet taste. They should be slit then added to soups and stews, so that their full flavour can be released. The Chinese believe that red dates are good for anaemics.

Rock sugar
Rock sugar is actually crystallised sugar sold in rock-like lumps. It is less sweet than granulated sugar.

Bean curd

Bean curd, made from soy beans, comes in many forms. Soft bean curd is sold as white squares or rectangles of curd immersed in water. There is also a circular type that is sold in plastic tubes, known as Japanese taufu. They should be able to keep for a few days. Bean curd cubes that have been fried in oil are called taufu pok.

Bean curd can be made into yellowish translucent sheets called bean curd sheets (foo pei). It is commonly used for wrapping meat and vegetable fillings. Make sure you buy the soft and flexible sheets because the brittle ones are inappropriate for wrapping.

Dried soy bean sticks (foo chok) are yellow in colour. They are often used in mixed vegetable dishes. They have to be soaked in warm water prior to use.

Soft salted bean curd cubes (lam yee) are kept preserved in a brine and wine solution with chillies. They have a distinctive flavour and complements porridge very well.

Hot bean paste

This spicy sauce is a made from a mix of fermented soy beans and chillies. It is also known as chilli bean sauce or hot soy bean sauce.

Five-spice powder

Five-spice powder is made from a combination of star anise, cinnamon, clove, fennel and Szechuan peppercorn. It is readily available at supermarkets. You only need a small amount to season roasted and braised poultry or meat and to reduce the strong flavour of beef, lamb and fish.

Fermented black beans

Fermented black beans or black bean sauce is sold in small plastic packets. Made from salted and fermented black soy beans, they have a very strong flavour so it is best to use sparingly. Before using, soak them in water for 5-10 minutes then rinse and drain thoroughly. Fermented black beans are used in both meat and seafood dishes.

Gingko nut

It is a yellow almond-shaped nut commonly used as either a savoury stuffing or in sweet soups. It is quite firm but becomes soft and tender once it has been cooked. You can buy it shelled or unshelled. Before using, cut it open with a paring knife to remove the bitter centre vein. Gingko nut is believed to be good for asthma, coughs, weak bladders and urinary disorders.

Sesame seeds

In Chinese cooking, white sesame seeds are used either roasted or raw to make sweets and fillings, or as garnishing in savoury dishes. It is also sold in creamy paste form in supermarkets.

Rice

Rice is the staple food of the Chinese people. Long grained rice is of better quality so always use it when available. In addition,

Rice vermicelli

Rice is made into long thin strands of white dried noodles to make rice vermicelli. Before using, it has to be softened first, by soaking in water if stir-frying or by scalding briefly if adding to a soup.
old rice is preferred to new rice because it will not stick together when cooked.

Noodles

For the Chinese, the long length of noodles symbolises longevity. Chinese noodles are available in a variety of forms, from thin strands to thick broad ribbons and either fresh or dried. They vary in terms of taste and texture so you should only use the particular noodle called for in the recipe and avoid substituting. The commonly used ones are yellow noodles and egg noodles. Yellow noodles are made from flour, alkaline water and yellow colouring while egg noodles contain an additional ingredient of eggs.

Transparent noodle (tang hoon)

Also known as bean thread noodle, transparent noodle is a thin strand noodle made from mung beans. It is often used in vegetarian dishes and in soups. Before using, you should soak it in water to soften first.

Water chestnut

The water chestnut has a sweet taste and is firm and crunchy. It is available in both fresh and canned form. It is also available in powder form, which is used for thickening soups.

Soy bean paste (tau cheo)
Soy bean paste is available in 2 forms, as whole soy beans or in purée form. The paste is light brown in colour.

Salted cabbage (harm choy)
Salted cabbage is made by salting and pickling green stem vegetables. You should wash it thoroughly and soak it in water to reduce the salt content before use. It is most commonly used in duck soup but it can also be fried with meat.

Dried shrimps
These small shrimps are very flavoursome so they are usually added to vegetable and soup dishes to enhance their taste. They are dried so you need to soak them in water to soften and rinse before using.

Star anise
This is a brown coloured, star-shaped spice that is actualy the fruit of the oriental evergreen of the magnolia family which is native to China and Japan. It has a strong and distinctive smell so all you need is a small amount to flavour meat, poultry and duck dishes.

Sour plums
These marble-sized, light brown plums have been pickled in vinegar and salt. They are usually used when steaming fish to add a sour tang.

INDEX